What people said ab
Marriage (Premarita

"God's Design For Marriage is the perfect book for preparing couples for marriage. It provides excellent content throughout, with stimulating discussion questions. My fiancée and I found the resulting deep conversations to be extremely fruitful, helping us build a strong and lasting foundation for our marriage. Too often, we spend years preparing for our vocation, months designing our new home, and weeks prepping for our next exam, but far less time preparing for marriage. If you are serious about wanting an incredible Christ-centered marriage then this is a must read."

—Ben, happily married husband

"Marriage preparation is so much more than knowing your future spouse's Myers Briggs type. This book helped me discover my expectations and my fiancé's expectations for marriage, then taught us what was realistic and biblical through discussions of God's purposes for marriage and what husbands and wives want/need from their spouse. I could not have been more prepared for marriage and even now, three years later, can't think of anything that this book missed. I am so thankful for this material!"

—Nicole, happily married wife

"If you are preparing for marriage or are someone who helps people prepare for marriage, I know of no better resource than this book. I have used it numerous times for pre-marital counseling, and I always ask the couples what they found most beneficial during our time of preparation. The answer tends to be split between two responses: the readings in the book and the questions in the book. Never my own personal advice and sage wisdom, but, oh well. The readings help couples understand the magnitude of what God is calling them to within the covenant of marriage. It also helps them face squarely the root problem of the overwhelming majority of marriage issues - our own sinfulness, but it does so within the context of abundant grace. The questions help them enter into marriage with a level of knowledge and understanding of each other that many couples who have celebrated their golden anniversaries never attain. This book, along with God's Word, Spirit, and grace give couples the vital foundation they need to have a marriage that fulfills its true purpose, to reflect Christ and His bride, the church."

—Todd, happily married pastor and counselor

"Due to the long distance nature of our relationship, my wife and I went through condensed premarital counseling. Despite this drawback, the contents of *God's Design for Marriage* reinforced ideas and teachings that our parents had instilled in us, as well as taught new Christ-centered ideas we have carried into our marriage. Be prepared to be challenged!"
—Caleb and Rachel, happily married couple

"In a culture that continues to diminish marriage, Doug Goodin provides a refreshing rebuttal in this book, vividly describing the Bible's high view of the marriage relationship. Doug clearly and cohesively lays out five purposes for marriage, with the central premise that marriage is designed for God's glory and your delight. My wife and I have had the privilege of walking through *God's Design for Marriage* with two engaged couples, and have found that this is not simply a stellar pre-marital counseling handbook, but also a wonderful post-marital resource. Both challenging and encouraging, it continues to help us cultivate our own marriage 'for His glory and our delight!'"
—Ben and Rosa, happily married couple and counselors

"What we appreciate about this book is its honesty and practicality. While there are other great books out there on different aspects of marriage, this book covers a broad spectrum of how to build a great marriage based unashamedly on biblical truths. Pastor Doug shows how "happily ever after" is not something found only in fairy tales or simply subject to the whims of emotions, but that every marriage can bring ever increasing joy to its participants when both spouses look to Christ and follow His example."
—Phil and Katie, happily married couple

"I would highly recommend *God's Design for Marriage*. It covers many vital topics that all soon-to-be-marrieds should consider and discuss. At the end of each section there are questions for the couple to talk about, which builds the habit of communicating about serious topics. I know our marriage is stronger because of what we learned through this book, and we continue to learn from it by revisiting it."
—Travis, happily married husband

"*God's Design for Marriage* never wavers from its biblical mooring. Pastor Doug offers wise and practical counsel to those who are considering marriage."

—Paul, happily married husband

"*God's Design for Marriage* has been extremely rewarding to each of us individually and as a couple. We really enjoyed the questions we had to answer. It was beneficial to see how we both felt about those topics as well as each other in specific situations. The biggest and most effective topic was *forgiveness* (how we need to forgive each other truly, and to mean it and not just say it). Also good was *flirting throughout the day* (extremely intriguing for later benefits!)."

—Joel and Tiffany, happily married couple

I have been through this personally in my own premarital counseling, and have used it to guide others through theirs. This material majors on the majors, getting to the heart of every must-cover marriage issue. It will probably make you squirm a time or two as hard topics are confronted: in-depth sin, roles in marriage, sex, and more, all from a Christ-centered and biblical perspective. It will also help you get to the practical level with some great application questions. It's the best I've seen on this incredibly important topic!

—Dan, happily married pastor and counselor

God's Design for Marriage (Married Edition)

Your Marriage Can Be Amazing!

Douglas Goodin

CROSS to CROWN
MINISTRIES

Douglas Goodin, *God's Design for Marriage (Married Edition)*

Copyright © 2017 by Douglas Goodin

Published by Cross to Crown Ministries
    5210 Centennial Blvd
    Colorado Springs, CO 80919
    www.crosstocrown.org

Cover design by Daniel Davidson, Colorado Springs, CO | www.bydan.us

Printed in the United States of America

ISBN: 978-0-9987863-0-8

To Krista,
the world's greatest wife,
who makes me happy to be married,
who gives me a taste of the heavenly feast every day.

Contents

Preface

There are two things you should know about the author of this book. First of all, he loves Jesus more than anything. He strives to live intentionally Christ-obsessed in every aspect of his life. I know because I am honored to have a front-row seat as God uses him, especially in premarital and marriage counseling. The Holy Spirit has given him an incredible gift to understand God's design for marriage. At times, I have been rendered speechless by the insights and conclusions he has seemingly pulled out of thin air.

The second thing you should know is that he loves me, and loves me well, almost as much as he loves Jesus. He has made it his business to really know me so he can love me even better. (I joke with people about reading their spouse's mind, but many times it seems as if Doug *can* read mine.) He has studied God's Word and worked hard to become a great leader and passionate lover. And he has taught me how to become a godly wife. Together, we enjoy romance, responsibilities, and everything in between.

You could look at it as though Doug wrote this book after 20 years of in-depth field study and experimenting — *on me!* — which means that the principles and practices you'll find in these pages are tried and true. I'm living proof.

To put it simply, my husband knows Jesus, and he knows marriage. That's why you should read this book.

Krista Goodin
Happily Married to the Author
February 14, 2017

How to Use This Book

There are two versions of this book, the *premarital edition* and the *married edition*. The one you are reading is the married edition. The content is largely the same in each, but this one has been tweaked and slightly expanded for married couples. The discussion questions have also been rewritten.

This book is intended to do three things: 1) teach you what the Bible says about marriage, 2) help you to understand each other's practical needs and wants, and 3) lead you into life-transforming conversations about your marriage. You will find some parts humbling and convicting, some parts stimulating and arousing. I hope you find all of it encouraging and Christ-glorifying.

Here are my simple recommendations to help you get the most out of this book:

1. Start at the beginning and take the chapters in order. (There is a design to their progression.)

2. Plan regular "discussion dates." When reading at home, be sure to eliminate distractions—put your devices away, turn off the TV, go to a private room. If you can, go out to a restaurant or coffee shop. Maybe take the book on a road trip or a weekend getaway. Be creative. Most of all, be consistent and go all the way through it.

3. Read together, out loud. Maybe take turns.

4. Read a section all the way until you get to a *Stop & Discuss* box. Talk through every question carefully before going on to the next section. (Be honest with yourself and with each other. Be gracious. Note any major disagreements, challenges, or problems, and seek help from a pastor or a couple with a good relationship who has been married at least 15 years.)

5. Pray together before and after each discussion date.

Marriage is one of God's greatest blessings when done the way He designed it. But it takes a lot of hard work to do it well. People sometimes suggest that Krista and I just got lucky or we must have it easy, that's why our marriage is so good. No, we just put in the effort to love each other the way Jesus told us to, and He faithfully brings the joyful intimacy He created it to bring. Your marriage can be amazing, too, if you're willing to do it His way.

So what are you waiting for? Get going! Read. Talk. Love.

Introduction

What do you think eternal life will be like? What says "paradise" to you? How would you describe it to someone?

Do you know how God describes it? As a glorious relationship of deeply satisfying, intensely passionate intimacy with Jesus in a place with no tears, no pain, no sorrow, and no death (Rev. 21). It sounds almost too grand to imagine, doesn't it? Yet He wants you to imagine it. Actually, He wants you to see it, hear it, feel it, smell it, and taste it. That is why He brought the two of you together as husband and wife. Did you know that?

God envisions heavenly rapture for your marriage, at least a glimpse of it. This is not to say that your marriage will ever be trouble-free. No, true paradise must delay until the next age because only then will the harsh consequences of sin be entirely destroyed. Still, God designed your relationship to give you each an experiential preview of the transcendent visage that awaits all believers in the new age. Your marriage should be the window through which you both peek into Heaven.

Does that sound impossible? After almost twenty-five years of firsthand experience, I can tell you that it is possible, *if you pursue marriage the way God designed it.*

Dare to Dream Big, Plan to Work Hard

Marriage was God's idea, not man's. We did not invent it, so it is not ours to adjust to suit our desires. We must "do it" the way He designed it.

But He did not design it to be drudgery. No indeed! The Almighty pictures an experience of unparalleled fulfillment, delight, pleasure, joy, and achievement together, not only because He loves us, but because He created marriage to be a living illustration of the relationship between Jesus and His Bride (the Church).

Consider the wedding night. It's the consummation of marriage. It's also one of the biblical metaphors for the bliss awaiting us when our King returns to consummate His kingdom. When that Day finally arrives, and we go to live together with our Beloved, it will most certainly *not* be the start of a long, boring, lifeless marriage. It will truly be *happily ever after.* Frankly, if your marriage is a dull, passionless, belligerent, strained, or painful relationship, it is a miserable example of a *Christian* marriage. Anyone who sees a Christian husband and wife together ought to find themselves aching for a similar experience of delight, fulfillment, and gratification.

Your ambition must not be for a *decent* marriage. Your sights must be set far higher. You should aim for the stars of marital rapture. You should look back one day to see that the honeymoon period was actually the *low* point of your marital satisfaction because as your faith matures, and as your love for each other grows, joy should intensify, not wane.

> *The Almighty's aim for marriage is a relationship of unparalleled fulfillment, delight, pleasure, joy, and achievement together.*

As you look at other marriages, you may conclude that such joy is rare. Maybe so, but you can have it if you both work hard and pursue your relationship as God intended.

In order to reach God's vision for your marriage, you have to study His design. Like everything else, it is found in His Word. My goal in this book is to present the Bible's teaching on marriage—applied through two and a half decades of personal experience and years of close pastoral involvement with other marriages—to help the two of you build a relationship that enjoys its intended happiness and fulfillment, so that you become an accurate picture of Christ and the Church, for His glory and your delight.

Stop & Discuss...

+ Think back, why did you want to get married? Tell each other.
+ Think of two or three marriages you want yours to be like. Why?
+ Think of two or three that you don't want to be like. Why?
+ Summarize the Bible's teaching about marriage as you understand it.

1

What Is Marriage?

Marriage As the World Sees It

Non-Christians generally have a low view of marriage. They see it as a relationship intended to bring fun and good times to people who travel through life together. That's really all it is—a mutually beneficial journey. So if one partner becomes unfulfilled or unhappy, or if someone else comes along who offers greater potential happiness, there is a good chance that the journey will end.

God did not design marriage to be like this.

Stop & Discuss...

+ Are you close to anyone who has been divorced? Discuss some of the difficult and painful consequences they experience as a result.
+ Why will *your* marriage not end in divorce?

Marriage As God Sees It

The Bible has a very high view of marriage as proven by the fact that when God expressed His love for Israel in the Old Covenant, He called them His wife. In the New Covenant, the Church is the "Bride of Christ." Your covenant relationship as groom and bride carries great significance, similar to God's covenant with His people.

Marriage Defined

George Bernard Shaw defined marriage as "an alliance entered into by a man who can't sleep with the window shut, and a woman who can't sleep with the window open." As true as that rings (in my house, at least), the Bible describes marriage first in terms of *covenant*.

Here are some biblical passages which speak of marriage using covenantal language (emphasis added):

"You were at the time for love; so I . . . swore to you
and **entered into a covenant** with you so that you
became Mine," declares the Lord God. (Ezekiel 16:8)

From the beginning . . . God made them male and
female . . . "The two shall become one flesh" . . . They
are no longer two, but one flesh. What therefore God
has **joined together**, let no man separate. (Mark
10:6-9)

The LORD has been a witness between you and the
wife of your youth . . . your companion and your
wife **by covenant**. (Malachi 2:14-17)

The adulteress who flatters with her words; that
leaves the companion of her youth, and forgets **the
covenant** of her God. (Proverbs 2:16-17)

A covenant is a contract, pact, or agreement where
two parties consent to be bound by predetermined
stipulations. Failing to abide by any of the stipulations
results in a breach of contract, a *broken* covenant. When
you entered into marriage, you were united together
under a binding contract, subject to predetermined
terms of agreement, accountable to God Himself until
one of you dies. *This is not to be taken lightly!*

For most people, a "binding contractual agreement"
sounds like a cold, business-like relationship. But that is
certainly not how the Bible speaks of it.

Consider the following passages (emphasis added):

For as a young man marries a virgin, so your sons
will marry you; and **as the bridegroom rejoices over
the bride**, so your God will rejoice over you. (Isaiah
62:5)

Let your fountain **be blessed, and rejoice** in the wife
of your youth. (Proverbs 5:18)

An excellent wife is the **crown** of her husband. (Proverbs 12:4)

He who finds a wife finds a **good thing**, and obtains **favor** from the LORD. (Proverbs 18:22)

An excellent wife, who can find? For **her worth** is far above jewels. (Proverbs 31:10)

The man said, "This is now **bone of my bones, and flesh of my flesh**; she shall be called Woman, because she was taken out of man. For this reason a man shall leave his father and his mother, and be joined to his wife; and they shall become **one flesh**. And the man and his wife were both **naked and were not ashamed**. (Genesis 2:23-25)

God uses language of rejoicing, intimacy, unity, blessing, preciousness, excellence, nakedness, and shamelessness when He speaks of marriage. There is nothing cold and business-like about that.

Furthermore, Malachi 2:14-17 and Proverbs 2:11-17 describe marriage as a "covenant of companionship." Why?

Do you remember how the creation account goes in Genesis 1 and 2? God had created land and sea, light and darkness, birds and fish, trees and flowers. Then He made the man Adam. After each stage of creation, God said, "It is good!" He was pleased with what He had made. But then God saw something that did not please Him—Adam was alone. This was "not good." His remedy? Eve. God made the woman so that the man would not be alone.

This means that you have been joined together in a *covenant of companionship*. Your marriage was created for friendship and intimacy between the two of you. So one of your marital goals must be to become close companions.

> *God uses language of rejoicing, intimacy, unity, blessing, preciousness, excellence, nakedness, and shamelessness when He speaks of marriage. There is nothing cold and business-like about that.*

You may not realize it, but the Bible begins and ends with marriage. The first Adam married his wife at the beginning of creation (Gen. 2), the last Adam will marry His wife at the beginning of the *new* creation (Rev. 21:1-4; 22:17). As bookends of God's story, marriage illustrates His committed, sacrificial, and eternal love for His people. Therefore, marriage must be highly esteemed by all and passionately pursued by those who are blessed to enter it.

Stop & Discuss...

+ Do you ever feel lonely? When? Why?
+ How is marriage designed to help?
+ What obstacles and sinful tendencies keep the two of you from being close companions with each other?

Vows

Earlier I defined a covenant as a contract where two parties are bound by predetermined stipulations. The stipulations of your marriage are the vows you made to one another during your wedding ceremony.

Because of the redefinitions of marriage taking place in our culture these days, it is important to understand that none of us are free to invent our own "terms of agreement." God defines marriage; He established your marriage requirements. So even if you did not *say* the traditional vows in your ceremony, you meant them, that is, you made the non-negotiable commitments which are captured effectively in the traditional vows. Our Lord takes vows very seriously, so must you.

Let's go through them as a reminder of what you promised to each other on your wedding day. The key statements are listed below along with a brief explanation of each.

"I take you to be my wedded husband/wife."

+ You did not get married under compulsion. No one forced you. You freely chose it because you wanted it. And you freely chose your partner. That is important to remember when things get tough. You should never think, "Was he/she really the one for me?" but "This is the person I committed myself to love and honor for the rest of my life no matter what happens." Your spouse is yours by choice.

"To have and to hold from this day forward."

+ *Having* and *holding* are shorthand expressions for close intimacy including both friendly companionship and sexual union. You agreed to seek these things with each other for the rest of your life. Many husbands and wives grow apart as the years go by because they stop pursuing each other relationally and sexually. Close affection of heart and body only happen with effort. On your wedding day you promised to make every effort to ensure that they happen throughout your marriage.

"For better or for worse."

+ There is no escape clause in your marriage contract. You took each other "as is." Or better yet "as will be" because whether one of you becomes a very different person than you now appear to be, or circumstances turn out quite differently than either of you had planned, the marriage commitment is valid and binding. You promised to love and honor each other in good times and in bad, come what may.

"For richer or for poorer."

+ This is the previous vow with a specific application—money. You promised to love and honor each other regardless of the size of your bank account. So whether you have to decide how to spend your millions or your pennies, your marriage contract requires unwavering devotion to each other.

"In sickness and in health."

- It may happen that in God's hard providence one of you will become unable to be the husband or wife that you both desire. Disease may render one of you bed-ridden, weak, or frail, incapable of earning a wage or of working around the house or of participating in life events or of engaging in sexual activity. Alzheimer's or dementia may strike. Chronic pain may prove debilitating. Infertility may emerge or any of a host of other mental or physical maladies, none of which will keep you from remaining faithful, true, and passionate about your spouse. *That* was your promise before God at the altar.

"To love and to cherish/respect."

- Husbands are called to love and cherish their wives; wives, to love and respect their husbands. *Cherish*, in the marriage context, means "to value highly." Husband, you pledged to treasure your wife above all other human relationships and above all other interests, hobbies, and loves. If at any point she becomes a lesser concern than your work, friends, children, family, or anything else, you will have become a covenant-breaker. Wife, you pledged to submit to your husband, affirming his authority over you, and admiring his efforts to care for you and your household. If at any point you treat him with contempt—as though he is under your authority—or disrespectfully, or rudely, you will have become a covenant-breaker.

"Till death do us part."

+ With two consequential exceptions (adultery and abandonment), the New Testament does not allow for divorce. Your commitment is for life. Notice that you did not commit to "stick it out for life," but to "keep these promises for life." It is not a matter of avoiding divorce, it is a resolution to make your spouse a happy, fulfilled, joyful husband or wife. You may stay married until death and yet fail to be a faithful partner by your negligence and lack of care for the other.

Remember, all of these oaths are before God. He is the one to whom you will one day give an account for your faithfulness.

Stop & Discuss...

+ What is the difference between asking, *Was he/she the one for me?* and asking, *Am I committed to love and honor this person for the rest of my life no matter what happens?*
+ Which vows seem easier? Which are harder? Why?
+ In your opinion, what are the main reasons why marriages fail to increase in love and passion?
+ Money is often ranked as the biggest marriage struggle. Why do you think that is?
+ Sex competes with money for the biggest marriage struggle. Why do you think that is?
+ Are you keeping your vows to one another? Are you willing to work harder at keeping them?

2

Picture (Husband)

The Five Purposes of Marriage

The Scripture reveals five purposes for marriage. I like to label them with 5 P's: *Picture, Pleasure, Purity, Providence, and Parenting.* You may think of others, but these are foundational and essential. We will consider them in this order.

A Picture of Christ and the Church

The New Testament uses several metaphors to describe the relationship between Jesus and the Church:

Jesus	Church
Foundation	Stones
Head	Body
King	Servants
Husband	Wife

An example of the last occurs when the apostle John saw the awe-inspiring visions of Christ in *The Revelation*:

> Let us rejoice and be glad and give the glory to Him, for the marriage of the Lamb has come and His bride has made herself ready. (Revelation 19:7)

And a little further,

> I saw the holy city, new Jerusalem, coming down out of heaven from God, made ready as a bride adorned for her husband. (Revelation 21:2)

The greatest use of the husband/bride analogy is in Ephesians 5:22-33. The husband is responsible to lead and love his wife like Christ leads and loves the Church. He should reflect the rule and care of Jesus. The wife is responsible to honor and follow her husband like Christians honor and follow Christ. She should reflect the humble submission of the Church. And so the unique roles of each partner are laid out through the verses of this section.

But at the conclusion, something quite astonishing happens. We are told that this Jesus/Church reflection is the supreme reason why God created marriage in the first place (v32). Do not proceed until you have grasped this point. If you miss it, you will miss the greatest reason for the existence of your marriage. Let me explain.

Verse 31 says,

> For this reason a man shall leave his father and mother and shall be joined to his wife, and the two shall become one flesh.

This is a direct quote from Genesis when God created the first marriage. A man and woman unite to form a new relationship, a new family, and a new life independent of their parents. Their bond is a covenantal commitment (as we have seen). Their bodies fit together deliciously like ice cream in a cone (as we will see). Their lives intertwine into a wonderful tapestry of purpose, love, and holy pursuits as they each fulfill their God-given responsibilities. From the beginning of creation, this is how God intended marriage to be.

Then comes verse 32:

> This mystery is great; but I am speaking with reference to Christ and the church.

Notice the word "mystery." In our day, a mystery is a puzzle to be solved or a secretive plot to be carried out by some unlikely villain awaiting discovery by a super sleuth such as Sherlock Holmes. But in the Bible, mystery is quite different. It describes *something formerly hidden that has now been revealed for all to see.* For example, in Ephesians 3, Paul explained that the

Gentiles' inclusion in God's redemptive plan was a mystery. It was intended from the beginning, and had been hinted at along the way through the Old Testament, but it was not fully known until the coming of Jesus and His New Covenant.

Marriage is another profound mystery. Its deepest meaning and purpose were hidden until the coming of Jesus. For thousands of years, the world thought it knew what marriage was about. They thought it was the foundation of the family and civilization, a relationship for raising kids and shaping culture. But God created it for a far greater and nobler reason. It is a real-life illustration of the relationship between God's Son and His people. That is its fullest and purest purpose which remained hidden until Jesus appeared. That's what Paul means when he calls marriage a "great mystery."

So your marriage is not first and foremost about forming a family or creating a culture. It's not primarily about living your dreams together or having a partner to handle the challenges of life with. No, your marriage is, above all, a picture of Jesus and His Bride the Church.

We might think of it this way: Jesus is the heart of God's plan for the universe. God the Father determined to give His Son a kingdom of people who would serve, honor, love, and please Him forever. He would be their greatest joy. The Son would lead them, protect them, provide for them, transform them, cherish them, and give His life for them because of His transcendent love. Jesus and His people would live together eternally in a relationship of great intimacy and joy. But before He set this grandiose plan in motion, He designed a prototype of what this glorious relationship would look like. He would create a man and a woman and give them a unique fellowship to simulate the coming fellowship between Jesus and the Church. The husband would play the role of Jesus, acting as leader, protector, and lover. The wife would play the role of the Church, acting as follower, helper, and admirer. Together they would be the foreword and introduction of the greatest Love Story ever written.

After many years of teaching and counseling, I would say that this is by far the least appreciated aspect of marriage. Which is like forgetting that the joy of a piano is making beautiful music.

Stop & Discuss...

+ Many couples have never really pondered what Paul said in Ephesians 5:22-33. Before going on, take a few minutes to read it. Identify and discuss how husbands are to be like Christ and how wives are to be like the Church. Talk about the mystery of marriage as a picture of Jesus and His people, and how marriage should reflect it.

Ephesians 5:22-33 is so important for marriage that we must go carefully and slowly through it. Let's begin by reading a portion of it again:

> Husbands, love your wives, just as Christ also loved the church and gave Himself up for her, so that He might sanctify her, having cleansed her by the washing of water with the word, that He might present to Himself the church in all her glory, having no spot or wrinkle or any such thing; but that she would be holy and blameless. So husbands ought also to love their own wives as their own bodies. He who loves his own wife loves himself; for no one ever hated his own flesh, but nourishes and cherishes it, just as Christ also does the church, because we are members of His body. (Ephesians 5:25-30)

A Big Little Word

Three times in the quote above the little word *as* occurs. Locate them. Circle them.

Do you know what *as* means? It introduces a comparison. If I say, "Gabe is as quick as a rabbit," I am comparing the running speed of my son with that of a bunny. The Ephesians quote compares three things which ought to make every husband sit up and take note:

1. Your love for your wife must be comparable to Christ's self-sacrificing love for the Church.

2. You are obligated to love your wife with actions comparable to the ways you love yourself.

3. You must nourish and cherish your wife comparable to the way Christ nourishes and cherishes Christians.

For His glory and our delight . . .

Husband, if that does not feel like an overwhelming, nearly impossible task, you do not yet understand what is required of you. Your love for her is to be "just as" Jesus loves you. You will know you are getting it when you begin to think that it might be easier to swim to the moon than to love someone like that.

As Christ Loved the Church

Notice that it does not say, "Love your wife as other men love their wives" or "Love her from the bottom of your heart" or "Love her like you want to be loved." Paul has specific comparisons in mind with specific goals and outcomes. You are to love your wife:

- ✦ **"As Christ gave Himself up for her."** Obviously, you cannot give your life as an atonement for your wife's sins. So, what is the comparison? It is found in the following phrases.

- ✦ **"That he might sanctify her."** Christ's death separated us from the evil world around us. He made us different. He made us holy. That must be your goal for your wife. You must spend your life working toward her sanctification. And it will cost you. You will feel, at times, as though you paid with your life. (We'll take a deeper look at this later.)

- ✦ **"Having cleansed her by the washing of water with the word."** The word of Christ is the *means* by which He sanctified the Church. It is also the means by which you sanctify your wife. The cleansing, purifying, refining gospel must be your primary instrument for washing your wife. You must constantly point her to Jesus, lead her to Jesus, remind her of Jesus, and bathe her in Jesus. You must show her the grace of the gospel, teach her the grace of the gospel, and immerse her in the grace of the gospel. You must ensure that she is growing and maturing in her trust of Him. This is *your* job. You are accountable to Him for your efforts toward her sanctification.

✦ **"That He might present to Himself the church in all her glory."** Christ's ultimate objective for the Church is for her to become radiant in beautiful holiness. That must also be your ultimate objective for your wife. Whatever ethical, moral, and spiritual blemishes exist in her right now fall to you to see that they are removed. Pause for a moment to let this Herculean task sink in.

> *The husband would play the role of Jesus, acting as leader, protector, and lover. The wife would play the role of the Church, acting as follower, helper, and admirer. Together they would be the foreword and introduction of the greatest Love Story ever written.*

Stop & Discuss...

+ Have you observed husbands sacrificing for the benefit of their wife? Did your fathers do it for their wife?
+ Do you know a husband who works hard to help his wife grow in obedience to Jesus? Did your father do that? What does this look like in marriage?

A Husband Is the Head of His Wife

At this point, husband, you may be mounting a protest thinking, "I can't sanctify my wife, that's God's work!" Well, you're right. And you're wrong. It is true that you cannot sanctify your wife, yet you must. *It's a command.* Confused? Stay with me. It will become clearer.

It seems that whenever the headship of husbands is brought up, the topic immediately shifts to what *wives* are not permitted to do or to be. However, before we discuss the roles of wives, we must be clear on what headship means for the man. Being the head of a woman is primarily concerned with what a *husband* must be and do. Husband, the standard is extremely high for you. Christ Himself is your role model. What does male headship look like? It looks like Jesus.

Consider how Christ exercises headship over the Church—He takes care of Her as His own body. You must regard your wife as your own body. That is precisely the imagery used throughout this text. The man who loves his wife loves himself because she is one with him. She is his body. This is the "one flesh" metaphor. I should think of my wife Krista as "the body of Doug."

What did Christ do for His body? He rescued it from destruction. He died on the cross to atone for its sins. He separated it from every other body. He cleaned it up, washing away its filth. When He finishes the purifying process, she will be a flawless form—no mars, no nicks, no imperfections whatsoever.

The apostle then says, "So husbands ought also to love their own wives as their own bodies." "So" is another little word with huge ramifications. *In the same manner* that Christ loves His body, men ought to love theirs. That is, men should observe how Jesus treats His Wife, and treat theirs accordingly. His goals for His wife must be your goals for yours.

Obviously, there is a limit to the analogy. I cannot atone for my wife's sins. It would not do her any good for me to hang on a cross because I am not a worthy sacrifice. I myself am in need of atonement, much less then could I redeem her (not to mention that fact that the eternal, perfect atonement has already been made). Nor can I autonomously and independently sanctify her or perfect her. However, by the grace of God, in the power of the Holy Spirit, I must try. That is my God-given responsibility for my wife. It is my privilege and duty to see to it that Krista becomes a clean, spotless, wrinkle-free, unique, faultless woman who brings glory to Christ by being my glory (1 Cor. 11:7). I must saturate her in the gospel of Jesus Christ. *I* must do it. I must work to present her as a perfect bride, as Christ does with His Bride.

Part of this mystery is that my bride is also His Bride, a good thing since I cannot actually change her. But Christ can.

We might imagine it like this. My wife is my garden. (Solomon called her that, but in an enticingly different context. We'll get to that later.) It is my responsibility to maintain a beautiful, fruitful garden. So I give it water and nutrients. I clear out the weeds and rodents. I cover it and protect it from the elements. I make sure it gets plenty of sunlight. Put simply, I do whatever it takes to make it wonderful. However, I don't control the rainfall or the sunshine. Ultimately, I do not have the wherewithal to make it a beautiful and fruitful garden. I depend upon Krista's *other* Husband, who happens to be the Lord of all creation, to do it. But it is still my responsibility. I must do my part, yet always with the understanding that it will produce nothing unless His power, His wisdom, and His will are also at work. I take it upon myself to bring my wife to holiness, and yet I will receive no glory if she makes it because, in the final analysis, it was really Jesus who did it. I can attach the hose and turn the faucet, but He is the one who makes and distributes the water. He is the one who causes the plant to grow. All glory to Christ! Yet, I must work.

> *You must constantly point her to Jesus, lead her to Jesus, remind her of Jesus, bathe her in Jesus. You must show her the grace of the gospel, teach her the grace of the gospel, immerse her in the grace of the gospel.*

Take this as an example. If I notice in Krista an attraction to gossip (which I do not, by the way), I should think to myself, *I've got work to do.* Now, if I were a young husband who had just learned that I am the head of my wife, I might simply point out her sin and demand that she quit immediately. However, over the years I've discovered that when removing a smudge from upholstery, a soft cloth works better than rough sandpaper. My approach should be like that of Jesus— gentle, gracious, and patient, yet intentional. Before anything else, I should take the matter before Christ and seek His help. It might also be prudent to seek the input of a few godly men who are a little further down the marriage path than me. I should consider several ways to address the issue. *Would a mentor be helpful? Does she have a solid grasp on what gossip is and why it is sinful? Are there good books that may help? Should I simply lay out directly what I have observed and express my concerns (being sure that it is expressed lovingly and kindly)?*

Whatever route I choose, I must be careful that my desire isn't to exercise my headship, but to move my wife closer to the righteousness that will please Christ. Again, when I see a flaw in Krista, I must not think,

How can she be like that? Rather I should conclude, *It's time to get to work, because her sanctification is my responsibility.*

Gossip is just one of many potential sins of your wife. Below are many more:

- ✦ She won't submit to you.
- ✦ She is not interested in Bible study, fellowship, worship, etc.
- ✦ She is aloof or unloving toward others.
- ✦ She is harsh with the kids, or negligent in parenting.
- ✦ She won't meet your sexual needs.
- ✦ She is disrespectful toward you.
- ✦ She is anxious and worried to the point of sin.
- ✦ She is bitter and angry toward you or others.
- ✦ She is self-centered and uncaring.
- ✦ She is lazy.
- ✦ She is materialistic, too concerned with worldly things.
- ✦ She is self-righteous or hypocritical.
- ✦ She is jealous or controlling.

The list could multiply, but you get the point. Your wife's sins are yours to correct.

Stop & Discuss...

+ Which aspects of "loving your wife as Christ loves the Church" explained here are new to either of you?
+ Husband, describe to your wife your responsibility regarding her sanctification.
+ Wife, what questions come to your mind as you learn all of this? How can this be scary? How can it be comforting?
+ Husband, how can you wash your wife with the gospel of Jesus Christ?
+ Look back at the list of potential sins and discuss how a husband might pursue his wife's sanctification for each of them.
+ Husband, do you love your wife enough to seek her glorification?
+ Wife, are you willing to let your husband seek your glorification?

How Do I Do It?

Good question. As I stated above, you can only do this by the grace of Christ and the power of His Holy Spirit. But since you do have a part to play, here are some suggestions to get you started.

1. **Know God's Word.** Your goal is to conform her to *His* image, not yours. Consequently, you must understand what He wants her to look like. The commands of Jesus are your marching orders. Study them well and incessantly.

2. **Know your wife.** You can't remove blemishes that you don't see, so you must study her. You must learn her weaknesses, struggles, temptations, and challenges. You must learn how to encourage her toward love and good deeds. You must make a habit of noticing how she acts and reacts. And you must consistently affirm and support her. You don't want the majority of your words to sound like criticism.

3. **Be intentional.** None of this will happen by accident. You must plan for it. Straight, healthy rows of corn do not grow naturally, they require purposeful work by the gardener. To be sure, your marriage consists of more than this duty to sanctify, but not less.

4. **Take a long-term view.** You don't have to remove every spot today. Showing up one evening with a stack of papers and saying, "I have made charts of all of your sins, listed alphabetically and categorized, and I want you to study them and eliminate them immediately," is not a very effective approach. That is not how Christ handles your sins. He is gentle and kind. He leads you gradually much of the time. When He does bring periods of "intense cleansing," He never overwhelms you with grief. He helps you

mature slowly and patiently. That is how you should approach your wife.

5. **Know your goal.** Remember, you are seeking her sanctification, not your headship. It's not about you getting to be in charge, it's about helping your wife become more faithful to Jesus. If you keep the real target constantly before your eyes, you will not slip into abuse against her. Every husband who uses his authority to injure his wife will give an account to the Lord for it. (And He's not going to like it.)

6. **Be gracious and patient.** Sanctification is a process for all of us. You haven't arrived at perfection yet, so don't expect too much from her. And don't be foolish enough to think she will always welcome and invite your correction. Let love cover a multitude of sins. Do your diligence and wait upon the Lord.

7. **Be humble.** One of the things that makes this assignment difficult is that the every husband has spots of his own. Husband, you are a sinner, too. This ought to keep you from ever being insensitive and overbearing with your wife. When I correct Krista, I do so knowing that there remains a great deal that needs correcting in me. This should make me a very humble "head of my wife."

8. **Seek the advice of others.** Especially seek men further down the marriage path than you. There is wisdom in many counselors. Do not naively think that you know what you are doing. You

have been given control of a rocket ship. Without help, you will crash to the earth destroying both you and her. With help, you may find yourselves exploring galaxies of joy beyond your wildest dreams. Ask for help, often.

9. **Pray.** Your greatest help will come from the Lord Himself. His strength, guidance, wisdom, love, and grace will equip you and enable you for this great task. Pray for your wife. Pray for your handling of her. Pray for self-control. Pray for the kind of love that Jesus has for His wife.

> When you see a flaw in your wife, you must not think, *How can she be like that?* Rather, *It's time to get to work because her sanctification is my responsibility.*

Two Dangers to Avoid

1. Neglect.
2. Browbeating, abuse of power.

Both are terrible sins against your wife. Both are terrible sins against your Lord. He is your example. He is neither timid nor tyrannical. He gently, but faithfully, works for your transformation. Be like Jesus.

Word to the Wife

Wife, you need to be willing to be loved in this way. It requires humility. It requires trust in Jesus, knowing that ultimately He is watching over you and transforming you. Because you want to submit to His tender love, you will submit to your husband's attempts to help you. If you refuse, not only will you be sinning against the One who commanded it, you will also slow your progress in sanctification. Allow Jesus to purify you through the man He gave you to represent Him.

Like Your Own Body

Men, let's face it, we love our bodies. I don't mean that we all love the shape of our body, I mean we show love to our body. We give our body what it wants. When I get up in the morning and my body wants a cup of coffee (or two), it gets coffee. When I pass by a Dairy Queen and my body wants a medium Reese's® Peanut Butter Cup Blizzard (okay, maybe a large), often I give it what it wants (probably too often). When my body wants to stretch out on the sofa with a glass of ice tea and a good book, that's where I put it.

Then there are those guys who care a lot about the look and health of their bodies. They show body-love by limiting its intake to fruits and vegetables. And chicken. They spend hours each week jogging and pumping iron. They pay for vitamin supplements and protein shakes. They take good care of themselves trying to avoid health problems, obesity, and the like.

So whether it's going for a walk, hitting the golf course, siting in the easy chair, watching football, eating a piece of blackberry cobbler, or napping in the shade, we men strive to please ourselves. It's just that simple.

With that in mind, read the following instruction:

> So husbands ought also to love their own wives as their own bodies. He who loves his own wife loves himself. (Ephesians 5:28)

Husbands are to "love their own wives *as* their own bodies" (there is that big little word again), which means that how we please ourselves becomes the standard for how we please our wife. Or to put it another way, husband, when you do more to make yourself happy than to make your wife happy, you disobey Jesus. You should make choices to please your wife *in the same way* that you make choices to please yourself.

There is a qualification to this command which we will consider later, but for the moment you need to grasp this principle—*Your wife should never receive less devotion than your body*. A righteous man does not love himself better than he loves his wife.

Husband, how much do you love yourself? How do your choices demonstrate your self-love? When you are hungry do you find food? Do you get food that you like or food that you don't? When you are sleepy or tired, do you provide rest for yourself? How about when you hurt, do you seek relief? Do you buy clothes that are ugly and uncomfortable? In how many ways do you love yourself? In all of those ways you should love your wife.

The impetus for this love comes from the fact that we are a picture of Christ and the Church. Think about this. The Church is Christ's body. We are in Him (1 Cor.

1:30) and He is in us (Col. 1:27). We are one with Him, members of His body. We are one flesh with Him (Eph. 5:31-32). He loves and takes care of His body. He does what benefits it. He blesses it. He serves it (Mark 10:45). In fact, everything that takes place in the world is done for the good of His body (Rom. 8:28). Marriage is given to picture this relationship. Therefore, in the same way that Christ loves His body, husbands are called to love theirs.

> *A righteous husband does not love himself better than he loves his wife.*

It Will Cost You

Such love comes at a price. In his book *Trusting God*, Jerry Bridges astutely declares, "One of the essential characteristics of love is the element of self-sacrifice." For example, all of the sanctifying responsibilities we discussed in the previous section takes time and energy which could be spent on something else. You must sacrifice them for the benefit of your wife. Money spent on her is money that could be spent on *you*. Virtually any expression of love takes something that could have been used to bring you satisfaction. Self-sacrifice is the offering required of husbands for the good of their wives. Husband, do you love her like this?

Here is a practical example of how this works in everyday life. When one man calls another man, he expects to be listened to attentively, as though the conversation is not a burden. He will be rightfully offended if the other guy is giving his attention to someone or something else. Nobody wants to hear the rapid clicking of a keyboard in the background interspersed with various combinations of, "Uh huh," "Mmmm hmmm," "I see," or "You don't say." This kind of thing irks a man. Yet, that same irked man will go home to his wife and watch TV, read, surf the internet, or stare off into space *while his wife talks to him*. This should never happen. Men are insulted when this happens to them. They should not do it to their wife.

I have a friend who disappears every day during his work breaks. One afternoon, a co-worker asked where he goes all the time. My friend replied, "I go to call my wife." The inquirer responded, "Hmmm, I've never had a wife who was worth my break time."

Is it any wonder that he has had more than one wife? (Somebody warn the next one before it's too late!) Yet many husbands, even good ones, are regularly tempted to belittle their wife when she calls, wanting her to get to the point quickly because he's got stuff to do. More important stuff. Now let's think about that. Your wife—the woman who has given her life, her future, and her body to you, the person to whom you promised unending love and adoration "till death do you part," the girl with whom you were so enraptured on your wedding day—this woman calls, and you want her to hurry up so you can get back to your computer screen? (More likely, you never took your eyes off the screen. You just wish she would hang up so you can use both hands on the keyboard.)

A man would never tolerate being "listened to" like that. We expect far greater treatment for ourselves.

Sadly, we often fail to perceive the lack of attention we give to our bride. We regard her calls or conversations to be bothersome (a message she hears loud and clear). Here is a hint: If you start to wonder whether your wife will *ever* stop talking, or *ever* say something really worth listening to, or *ever* consider how much you have to do and maybe back off for a while, you are treating her with contempt. You are sinning against her by regarding her to be inferior to yourself. If she treated you that way, you would be humiliated. Guess what? So is she! She is your body, your own self. Treat her accordingly. It is the command of sacred Scripture.

> *Self-sacrifice is the offering required of husbands for the good of their wives.*

Nourishing and Cherishing

> For no one ever hated his own flesh, but nourishes and cherishes it, just as Christ also does the church, because we are members of His body. (Ephesians 5:29-30)

Two words every husband must memorize and master are *nourish* and *cherish*. It would be an oversimplification, but I am tempted to say that together they represent the husband's entire job description.

A husband holds two relational positions with his wife. One is vertical, the other horizontal. The vertical is his authority as head, almost a father-figure. The horizontal is his partnership, friendship, and camaraderie with her. *Nourish* and *cherish* capture these two relationships.

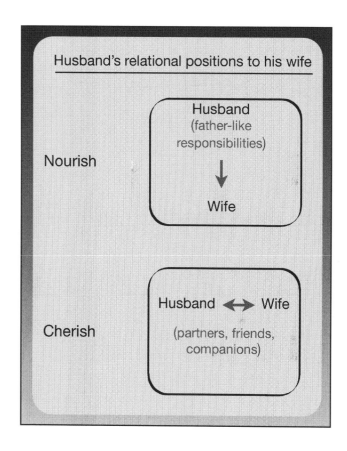

Nourish has to do with the husband's father-like authority and responsibility. It means "to feed" or "to bring up a child." The husband is expected to provide for the physical and temporal needs of his wife in the same way that her father should have done when she was growing up. The transfer of responsibility from the father to the husband is represented in the traditional wedding ceremony when the officiant asks, "Who gives this woman to be married to this man?" and the father responds with, "Her mother and I." The groom now assumes the task of supplying the woman with housing, food, clothes, etc. He is also expected to provide her with security (which will be discussed in much more detail later) and whatever is needed to grow in maturity as a person, woman, wife, and mother. Husband, all of this and more is yours to supply to your wife.

Cherish means something like "to value highly." We cherish things we consider precious and special. Guys cherish different things: their car or bike, an autograph or a signed picture of their favorite player, their father, brother, or best friend. Whatever we cherish, we take great care of and spend time with.

When Krista and I were first married, I worked at a music store. My primary responsibility was the acoustic guitar section. One guitar, a *Guild*, captured my attention. I tuned and cleaned that guitar every day for hours. It was one of the sweetest sounding instruments I had ever heard. My affection for it grew to the point that I would not show it to customers for fear they might buy it. One day, the owner of the store told me that he was dropping the *Guild* line. All the guitars were to be packed up for shipping away. That night, I took Krista out to dinner and told her the devastating news. But, I had a plan. I would buy the guitar. Even with my significant employee's discount, it stretched our budget. Nevertheless, with Krista's support, I bought it.

Over the next several years very few hands touched that guitar. I polished it frequently, kept it well-strung and tuned, washed my hands thoroughly before playing it, and required those who *were* allowed to play it to do the same. No one was to hold it while wearing a belt-buckle which might scratch its pristine finish. When I was not playing it, it lived securely and comfortably in a hardshell case stored safely out of harm's way. The high value I placed upon that guitar was demonstrated by my actions.

This is how a husband should view his wife. Not that she should be encased and stored away in a safe place, but similar time, care, attention, and protection should be evident. A wife should be convinced that she is the single most important possession (so to speak) that her husband owns. Husband, your wife should feel like your most prized treasure, so adored that nothing else and no one else even comes close. More than your time, pet, friends, car, books, hobbies, family, goals, job, guitar…more than everything, *she* is your obsession.

She will only *feel* treasured in this way if she really *is* so treasured by you. In other words, she will not feel cherished unless you sincerely cherish her. It cannot be faked or stumbled upon. It is shown (or not) by your attitudes and actions, moment by moment, day by day. It comes out in the decisions you make, how you spend your time and money, where you live, and so on. It includes big things and little things.

It is especially evident when you choose things that she knows you do not particularly like. For example, I hate cats. As a pastor-theologian who knows Greek and Hebrew, I can tell you with authority that cats were not part of the original good creation. God did not create them; Satan did. They rose out of the pit after the Fall and will perish with him and his demons. (Okay, I admit it, I made some of that up.) However, I love my wife. So on Valentine's Day some years ago, I bought her not one but two cats. I paid for their shots, food, and collars. I turned a deaf ear to their incessant meowing and a blind eye to their marring of our best furniture. I resisted every urge to torture them. (Okay, not *every* urge. But the little imp deserved it. Really. What could I do? It was my righteous duty before God....) Why did I do this? Because I value my wife and want to make her happy. To show that I treasure her above myself, I invited those diabolical beasts into our lives. By this action, she knew I loved her.

A Marriage Maxim

Brother, let me tell you something which can make you a very happy man (and your wife a very happy woman). It's simply this: *A cherished woman wants to please her husband*. Memorize that and believe it. It will be the difference between marital bliss and marital blah.

There are endless ways for a husband to cherish his wife. We will consider some of them later. For now, you must firmly grasp that you (husband) are to treasure your wife the way Christ treasures the Church. He does not always give us what we want, but He always gives us what we need. And He makes us feel worthy of His self-sacrifice. Moreover, He lavishes every good gift upon us, freely giving us all things, culminating in the joy of eternal life with Him in the paradisal new earth.

That is the pattern for husbands to follow in cherishing their wives.

Your Marriage as a Picture

Husband, if we were to use your marriage as the portrait of Jesus and His bride, what would we learn about Christ?

+ Does your marriage display Jesus as a harsh, abusive, and domineering husband?

+ Do you show the world that Jesus only blesses His wife when He expects to get something in return?

+ Do you display a Jesus who would rather watch football, read a book, go fishing, or surf the Web than spend time with the Church?

+ Do you reveal a Jesus who considers it a bother when the Church asks for help?

+ When people look at your marriage, do they get the idea that Jesus would really rather be married to someone else, someone taller or thinner or more interesting or more intelligent or with significantly enhanced physical features?

+ Do you portray a Jesus who cannot keep His eyes off of other women?

+ Do you show a miserly Jesus who will not spend money on gifts or vacations or getaways for His wife, but somehow finds the cash for new toys or computers or golf for Himself?

+ Do you show a Jesus who leaves leadership and responsibility to the Church?

+ Do unbelievers learn from your marriage that Jesus has more important things to do than listen to the requests, concerns, and dreams of the Church?

+ Do you reveal that Jesus criticizes every little thing the Church does wrong and points out all of her flaws?

+ According to your relationship, when Jesus corrects the Church does He leave her bruised, discouraged, and feeling worthless?

+ Do people see a Jesus who is involved in a lot of really good things, but rarely has time for the Church? That He will spend more time with the Church "as soon as He has more time"?

Or . . .

+ Does your marriage display that Jesus is doing everything for the benefit of the Church?

+ That Jesus is committed to loving and caring for His bride?

+ That Jesus is patient and kind to the Church?

+ That Jesus considers the Church His most precious possession?

+ That Jesus would never do anything to hurt or frustrate or discourage the Church?

For His glory and our delight . . .

+ That Jesus is always happy and interested to hear the Church's concerns?

+ That Jesus is gracious with the Church's faults and does not become angry at her failures?

+ That Jesus treats the Church well even when she does not please Him?

+ That Jesus leads, directs, protects, and provides for the Church?

+ That there is no sacrifice that Jesus will not make for the Church?

+ That Jesus is tenderly kind and endlessly compassionate toward the Church?

These are hard questions for any husband, but they are worth extensive reflection not only because of the vows we made to our wife regarding cherishing and nourishing, but also because a bad marriage lies to the world about the character of Jesus. It presents a distorted picture of His love for His bride. Every husband reflects Christ. We either reflect Him accurately or we present a caricature, but either way we present Christ. We should strive to be copies which are as true to the original as possible. Husband, love your wife like Christ loves the Church.

Stop & Discuss...

+ Describe how a husband and wife have both a vertical and horizontal relationship.
+ Define *nourish* and *cherish*. How does Christ nourish and cherish the Church?
+ Wife, what does your husband place a high value upon? How does it show?
+ Husband, what makes your wife *feel* cherished? Wife, is he right?
+ Husband, what things are you willing to sacrifice in order to love your wife? Is there anything you are unwilling to sacrifice for her?
+ Wife, when talking on the phone, does it ever seem as though you are bothering him? Or face-to-face, does he "go other places" in his mind while you are talking? If so, how does it make you feel? Explain it to him.

3

Picture (Wife)

Wives, be subject to your own husbands, as to the
Lord. For the husband is the head of the wife, as
Christ also is the head of the church, He Himself
being the Savior of the body. But as the church is
subject to Christ, so also the wives ought to be to
their husbands in everything. (Ephesians 5:22–24)

The Wife's Part of the Picture

The first command given for marriage is that wives
must submit to their husbands.

I can hear the drums pounding off in the distance.
The mood has intensified. The light has dimmed. The
ground is pulsating beneath my chair as they march. It's
the orcs coming to destroy me for daring to even utter

the word *submission*. It's worse than predestination, more repugnant than Hell. It has to be a mistake. God would never put that word in the Bible. Surely the Greek has been twisted and distorted by some medieval chauvinistic scholar who hated his mother. It's degrading! It's hate-speech! It's inhumane! Paul hates women! No wonder he didn't have a wife. He would never be brave enough to suggest such a thing if he were married!

Okay, so maybe I'm laying it on a little thick. But there are those who get this fired up and more so at the thought of a woman being told to submit. Nevertheless, we who love Christ must submit to Him regardless of what others think or say.

God's Definition of Submission

Let's define our terms. The Greek word for submission ('subjection' is a synonym) is *hupotasso*. It is a compound word with the root (*tasso*) meaning "to put or to place" and the prefix (*hupo*) meaning "under." Therefore, 'submit' is "to put or place under." When a woman gets married, she places herself under the authority of her husband. It is *her* decision, a permanent one.

So the command of 5:22 is, "Wives place yourselves under the authority of your husband." This is not good advice or a good suggestion. It is a command. It *must* happen in marriage. A wife must place herself under her husband's authority.

To submit is to obey. Those who teach submission is not the same as obedience argue from an agenda, not from the Bible. In 1 Peter 3:5-6, Abraham's wife Sarah is given as a wonderful example of submission because she "obeyed Abraham, calling him lord." That is what it means for a wife to place herself under her husband. Her obedience is "as to the Lord" (Eph. 5:22). And notice the little word *as* again. A wife's submission to her husband should be similar to her submission to Jesus. Obviously her husband is not Jesus, and she should not worship him. Yet the command is plain—a wife is to obey her husband as she would Christ.

Contrary to modern, humanistic opinion, there is nothing inherently undignified about being in submission to someone else. Jesus submitted to Mary and Joseph when He was a boy (Luke 2:51). Imagine that! The Son of God placing Himself under the authority of sinful humans. (And without a single cry of protest and outrage.) Later, Jesus openly testified that He was under the authority of His heavenly Father and sought only to do His will (i.e. *to obey*). Was Jesus inferior or repressed by letting God the Father call the shots? Of course not. In 1 Corinthians 15:28, the Son Himself—the glorified Messiah, ruler of heaven and earth—will again be "subjected" to the Father. It is the same word used here to describe wives. Jesus will be placed under the authority of God the Father, and in that subjugation He will not lose one iota of worth, dignity, or even, deity.

Being under a higher authority does not make a person a lower form of being, it simply makes him or her under authority. A wife equals her husband in value and worth, but she is under his authority.

Also note that wives are not commanded to be submissive to *all* husbands, but to their *own*. My wife does not have to obey every man that comes along. She has not placed herself under them but under me. She is not Krista Johnson or Krista Williams or even Krista Goodwin. She is Krista Goodin. She has taken *my* name and has pledged her obedience to *me* alone.

> *There is nothing inherently undignified about being in submission to someone else.*

The Why and How Far of Submission

Why should a wife submit to her husband?

> For the husband is the head of the wife, as Christ also is the head of the church. (Ephesians 5:23)

Wives are half of the Christ/Church picture in marriage. They play the part of the Church who loves Christ by obeying Him. Jesus said it like this, "If you love me, you will keep my commandments" (John 14:15). Christians who claim to love Jesus but refuse to obey Him show that their claim is an empty one. Christians must obey Christ. This obedience is to be depicted by a wife's compliance with her husband's will.

What is the extent of this submission? In what areas of life must she submit? Where can she draw the line? Paul answers these questions, too. He made it very simple:

But as the church is subject to Christ, so also the wives ought to be to their husbands *in everything*. (Ephesians 5:24, emphasis added)

Wife, what aspects of living and decision-making are not part of "everything"? Those are the things in which you do not have to submit.

There is, of course, one exception to "everything." If a husband were to command what God prohibits or prohibit what God commands, then she must obey God and not her husband. For example, if a husband were to tell his wife to abort a pregnancy, the wife must have the baby against his will. Or if he told her not to go to church, she would have to reject that instruction. He may not force her to engage in sexual activity with others, or ask her to lie or join him in illegal activities, or anything else that displeases God. Put simply, a husband does not have the authority to demand that his wife sin. But asking a wife to do something she does not want to do is not the same as asking her to sin. A wife must be careful to keep that distinct or she will find herself disobeying Christ by disobeying her husband.

> *What aspects of living and decision-making are not part of "everything"? Those are the things in which you do not have to submit.*

Take Submission Seriously

We should remember that the apostle Paul did not invent the concept of submission. He did not awaken one day and think, "That sounds like fun! I'll tell all the slaves to obey their masters, children to obey their parents, and wives to submit to their husbands." No, the Holy Spirit of God inspired Paul's teaching.

The Spirit also commanded wives to obey "in the fear of Christ." The socially acceptable definition of *fear* in such passages is "reverence" or "respect." But to modern ears, I think this waters it down too much. I grant that believers must not walk around in a morbid state of terror when they think of Christ ("He has not given us a Spirit of slavery leading to fear," "There is no fear in love," etc.). However, a woman who claims to love Christ and yet obstinately refuses to do what He commands has every reason to fear Him. That hard-heartedness may indicate that she does not love Christ after all, in which case she will hear at the Judgment, not "Well done!" but, "Depart from Me, I never knew you" (Matt. 7:21-23). That is the fear of which the apostle speaks. Refusing to submit to one's husband equates to refusing to submit to the Lord Himself (see Eph. 6:5f). This is a terrifying thought, indeed.

My objective is not to hang a dark cloud over the heads of wives, but to ensure that we understand what is at stake here. The Bible's authority has been greatly undermined and damaged by the influence of liberalism and feminism. We too easily gloss over such stern and sober assertions to our detriment. Paul is not ambiguous. He affirms, candidly, that submission is serious and must be entered into with the clear understanding of Who stands behind the command.

Wife, please listen to this advice. When you said "I do" to your husband, you not only agreed to enjoy all the fun and romance with him, you also said, "I place myself under your authority and will submit to you for the rest of my life. May the Lord Jesus deal with me if I fail to submit to you."

Submission in Practice

Let me conclude this section with a few practical comments. First, to be in subjection does not mean that the wife has no input into decisions. Marriage is not a master/slave relationship. It is good and right for a wife to share her thoughts and opinions. That's what companions and partners do. Any husband with an ounce of sense will seek his wife's contributions and appreciate her wisdom.

Wife, there is nothing disrespectful about offering suggestions, if you offer them *respectfully*. Yet when the discussion comes to an end with the two of you in disagreement, you must submit. Joyfully. Willingly. Giving full support to his decision. Refusing to say (or think), "I told you so" when it turns out that yours was the wiser choice (and it will sometimes). If your husband makes a turn that will put you in the ditch, after offering your alternate recommendation you go with him into the ditch without complaint. And then you help him get back out without condescension.

Second, a submissive wife is no fragile flower too weak or delicate to be of any use. Think of the Proverbs 31 woman. She is amazingly talented and adventurous. She is robust and active. She is relentless and spry. And she is utterly submissive to her husband. She represents the Church's devotion to Christ with exceptional grace and propriety. Strive to imitate her. (We will study her in detail later.)

Third, your respect of your husband will be most evident in your mouth. That is, what you say will either convey respect or disrespect more than anything else you do. Anytime you talk down to him, speak critically of him, speak critically *to* him, raise your voice at him, rebuke him as though he is under *your* authority, or belittle him, you commit sin. You should never speak to your husband in a way that you would not speak to the Lord, because your submission is "as to the Lord."

> *Refusing to submit to one's husband equates to refusing to submit to the Lord Himself.*

Your Marriage as a Picture of the Church and Christ

Wife, if we were to use your marriage as the portrait of Jesus and His bride, what would we learn about the Church?

+ Does your marriage teach that sarcasm and criticism are appropriate ways for the Church to speak to Christ?

+ That the Church should strive to look good while others are watching, but with Christ she gets to "relax" and "let her guard down"?

+ That it is right and appropriate, at times, for the Church to order Christ around acting as *His* authority?

+ That the Church is faithful to Christ in body, but her mind and heart belong to another?

+ That when Christ fails to do things the Church's way, she should belittle him to all her friends?

+ That the Church is free to have unspoken expectations and be upset at Christ for not meeting them?

+ That the only way the Church will motivate Christ is by constantly nagging and complaining?

+ That the Church was captivated by Christ early on, but somewhere along He became less admirable?

+ That if the Church is in a bad mood or hormonal, she does not have to treat Christ with kindness and respect?

+ That the Church has it okay, but Christ is not as good a husband as other men she knows?

Or . . .

+ That the Church has great reverence and admiration for Christ?

+ That the Church is grateful for the many things Christ does to show His love for her?

- ✦ That because Christ is her head, the Church is careful to speak kindly and respectfully to and about Him?

- ✦ That the Church loves Christ with all her heart, soul, strength, and mind?

- ✦ That when Christ makes decisions, the Church accepts them with trust and patience?

- ✦ That when the Church speaks of Christ, she is careful not to say anything that would tarnish his reputation?

- ✦ That the Church's primary goal is to bring glory to Christ and honor Him in private and in public?

Wife, a good marriage shows the world how much the Church honors Christ. Do your part to paint an accurate picture.

Stop & Discuss...

+ Wife, define *submission*.
+ Discuss together how well or poorly your mothers submit to their husband.
+ Wife, what is most difficult about submitting to your husband? Why?
+ Wife, does submission provoke emotion inside you (fear, anger, jealousy, doubt)? Explain.
+ Why is submission not the same as helplessness, weakness, or inferiority?
+ Husband, does your bride ever speak to you in a way that feels disrespectful? Tell her about it.
+ Wife, are you willing to obey the commands of this man? Why or why not?

4

Pleasure

Introduction

Read again what I wrote in the Introduction:

> God envisions heavenly rapture for your marriage, at
> least a glimpse of it. This is not to say that your
> marriage will be trouble free. No, true paradise must
> delay until the next age because only then will the
> harsh consequences of sin be entirely destroyed. Still,
> your wedding day and every day after are designed
> to give you each an experiential preview of the
> transcendent visage that awaits all believers in the
> new age. Your marriage should be the window
> through which you both peek into Heaven...The
> Almighty pictures an experience of unparalleled
> fulfillment, delight, pleasure, joy, and achievement

together, not only because He loves us, but because He created marriage to be a living illustration of the relationship between Jesus and His Bride (the Church). Consider that the wedding night is one of the biblical metaphors for the bliss awaiting us when our King returns to consummate His kingdom. When that Day finally arrives, and we go to live together with our Beloved, it will most certainly *not* be the start of a long, boring, lifeless marriage. It will truly be *happily ever after*. Thus, a dull, passionless, belligerent, strained, or painful marriage is a miserable example of a Christian marriage. Anyone who sees a Christian husband and wife together ought to find themselves aching for a similar experience of delight, fulfillment, and gratification.

So, your ambition must not be for a *decent* marriage. Your sights must be set far higher. You should aim for the stars of marital rapture. You should look back one day to see that the honeymoon period was actually the *low* point of your marital satisfaction because as your faith matures, and as your love for each other grows, joy should intensify, not wane.

Alas, this seems so rare, so foreign to our thinking. Why? Is it because we are ignorant of God's design for marriage? Or because we are lazy? Or because we do not really believe that perpetual pleasure is possible in marriage? Or because we are unconvinced that God condones such an interest in earthly satisfaction? Or, worse still, that He opposes it?

In this chapter I hope to persuade you that God intends for you both to enjoy marriage abundantly.

The Wonder of Knowing and Being Known

One of the biblical expressions for sex between a man and his wife is that of "knowing" each other. Genesis 4:1 says (literally), "And the man *knew* his wife Eve, and she conceived" (emphasis mine). Why did God choose such a cognitive term (know) for such a physical act (sex)? You can be sure that it is no mere euphemism like the modern, "She slept with him" or "They spent the night together." God designed marriage to be a deep friendship climaxing in deep bodily communion between a man and a woman. It is made to be a transcendent love of the most profoundly intimate kind, which only comes when a person is profoundly *known*.

The psalmist spoke of such knowledge in Psalm 139:1-6 quoted below. As you read, put yourself in the place of the person being known:

> O Lord, You have searched me and known me. You know when I sit down and when I rise up; You understand my thought from afar. You scrutinize my path and my lying down, and are intimately acquainted with all my ways. Even before there is a word on my tongue, behold, O Lord, You know it all. You have enclosed me behind and before, and laid Your hand upon me. Such knowledge is too wonderful for me; it is too high, I cannot attain to it.

If you get the feeling that someone is constantly watching you, you have understood the passage correctly. That someone is God Himself. He searches you and knows every part of you, inside and out. He knows all that you think, want, say, and do. On some days, that may be comforting. On others, it can be somewhere between intimidating and terrifying. But notice what He does with that knowledge. He does not back away, close His eyes, or turn His head. He moves toward you. He surrounds you with Himself. He touches you. Why? Because He loves you. None of that knowledge, right up to the ugliest and most ridiculous parts, drives Him away. Because Jesus bore your shame on the cross, you can now be completely naked and unashamed before God. He is a safe place, even in your failures.

When you sense just how deeply He knows and loves you, you will experience something so profoundly wonderful that words cannot adequately articulate what you want to say. Marriage is designed to give expression to that wonder.

Now read it again and put yourself as the knower.

How do you gain such intimate knowledge of another person? You search, observe, ponder. You actively pursue it. You get close enough to see who he or she really is. You spend the time necessary to learn. True knowledge comes from studying what you love. If you study each other like this, your experience will truly become something too wonderful to describe.

Conversation

Today, *intercourse* is used almost exclusively to refer to sex. In days gone by, it was used predominantly to describe the verbal exchange of ideas, thoughts, and feelings between people or groups. I dare say that if husbands and wives take the time to enjoy satisfying intercourse in the older sense of the word, they will be more than satisfied with their enjoyment of it in the newer sense. We'll get to the sexual pleasure of marriage in a moment, but first consider the pleasure of conversation.

In my observation, many husbands and wives spend relatively little time talking with one another. Oh, they talk *at* each other, and give briefings when necessary to keep the family machine running. But unhurried, prolonged conversations would be nice "if we had the time." The time that could be spent talking is often given to the great intercourse-killers: TVs, computers, smart phones, tablets, and the like.

It wasn't always that way. I don't mean before the microchip. I mean earlier in their relationship, before they were married, when they couldn't get enough of each other. Parting was such sweet sorrow. The next encounter, even if the next day, seemed like an eternity away.

Remember your engagement? What did you spend most of your time doing? Talking, right? About everything. You were getting to know each other's likes, dislikes, tastes, desires, long-term goals, past experiences, and favorite ice cream flavors. You rarely took a breath. When you did, the pause was quickly filled with another question. Or maybe there was an extended period of quiet. That, too, was amazing because there was no one you would rather do nothing with. One would think that after the wedding, it would be more of the same only better because you never have to end the date.

But that rarely happens. Too often, couples get to a point where they think, *It seems like we are together all the time. I need some space. I need to get out once in awhile. Can't I have some time to myself to just watch some TV and relax? I need some downtime. I just need to veg right now, we can talk later.* But later rarely comes. For most couples it's always now.

Husbands and wives are "one flesh," "head and body," "groom and bride," and "co-heirs of eternal life." How can they *not* desire conversation with each other? It's because they become lazy, resentful, or bored.

> *I dare say that if husbands and wives take the time to enjoy satisfying intercourse in the older sense of the word, they will be more than satisfied with their enjoyment of it in the newer sense.*

You must always *work* at knowing each other, expending the energy necessary to answer questions like: *What kind of music does your husband like? What is your wife's greatest fear? Can you describe each other's most enjoyable experiences? Do you know what makes each other happy? sad? pensive? agitated? giggly? What is your husband's favorite hobby? Why does he enjoy it so much? What is God teaching our spouse these days? What is your wife's idea of a romantic date and when is the last time you made that happen? What goes on in her mind and heart when your mother comes to visit? Is your answer based on man's intuition or have you actually asked her about it? Does he struggle to pray and study the Bible on a regular basis? Why? What did her family do to celebrate Christmas and New Years? Does she want to continue those traditions or create new ones?*

The desire for discussion does not fade with time, especially for women. I know this from firsthand experience. After ten years of what we both agreed had been a happy, intimate, loving marriage, I asked Krista what would take it to the next level for her. Her answer was the last thing I expected. She said, "I would love it if I could have more of your undivided attention each week so that we could just talk about stuff." I know what that sounds like—like *I* was the happy one while she was starving for my attention. She assured me that that was not the case. It was simply that her desire to talk with me was intense (like most men's desire for the other kind of intercourse).

I determined to make the necessary changes in order to meet this need of hers. What I discovered was that I, too, found great pleasure in these conversations. More than that, I realized that this was not so much a *new* fire as a re-kindling of an old flame that once burned much brighter. During the early part of our marriage, spending time with Krista was my greatest desire. Sure, I had a multitude of interests and pursuits, and I managed to find time for them, but above all I wanted to be with her. It didn't really matter what we were doing as long as we were together. I wanted to know her, to discuss issues with her, to discover what made her tick (and tickled), to figure out how I could surprise her or impress her or bring her joy and happiness. Before marriage, after I dropped her off at home she would call my cell phone so we would talk until I got home, even if we had been together for ten or twelve hours. That is how much we enjoyed conversing with one another. We still do, and now we are making more time for it.

Also rekindled was my eagerness to bless Krista romantically. Early in our relationship, as my knowledge of her grew, my creativity in planning dates and purchasing gifts grew accordingly. Guess what! That creativity still exists, it just needed a new round of knowledge to awaken it from its dormant state. Now, over twenty years later, Krista is more interesting to me than ever. My desire to spend time with her is at an all-time high. Our conversations are more frequent and more meaningful than ever. We are truly finding one of the great pleasures of marriage to be intercourse, the talking kind.

You may need this kind of rediscovery, too. Commit yourselves to talking, studying, and learning about each other. Determine never to stop.

Stop & Discuss...

+ Who knows you better than anyone else? Describe that relationship and what it means to you.
+ Share something you have learned about the other recently.
+ Is there anything that keeps you from wanting to be truly known? Talk about it.
+ Why is it important to know each other deeply?
+ How much time do you spend weekly in intimate conversation? What can you change to make it happen more often?

Beauty

Because of the obvious pitfalls surrounding it, Christians often avoid discussing the beauty of the human body. We tend to think that any guy who notices another woman's form must be lusting after her. It is okay to observe how beautiful a woman's *dress* is, but he better not admit to having noticed the body in the dress.

There is good reason for being careful in this area. Taking in the new car smell of my buddy's new ride is fine for a few moments, but it can easily lead to coveting or discontentment toward what God has blessed me with.

Nevertheless, the Scripture does not shy away from expressing the physical, bodily appeal of men and women:

> When [Abram] was about to enter Egypt, he said to Sarai his wife, "I know that you are a woman beautiful in appearance." (Genesis 12:11 ESV)

> When Abram entered Egypt, the Egyptians saw that [Sarai] was very beautiful. (Genesis 12:14)

> "[Rebekah] was very attractive in appearance, a maiden whom no man had known." (Genesis 24:16 ESV).

> When you go out to battle against your enemies, and the LORD your God delivers them into your hands and you take them away captive, and you see among the captives a beautiful woman, and have a desire for her and would take her as a wife . . . . (Deuteronomy 21:10-11)

> Now the man's name was Nabal, and his wife's name was Abigail. And the woman was intelligent and beautiful in appearance . . . . (1 Samuel 25:3)

> Now Adonijah the son of Haggith exalted himself, saying, "I will be king," . . . and he was also a very handsome man. (1 Kings 1:5-6)

> So [Jesse] sent and brought [David] in. Now he was ruddy, with beautiful eyes and a handsome appearance." (1 Samuel 16:12)

> Now it was after this that Absalom the son of David had a beautiful sister whose name was Tamar, and Amnon the son of David loved her. (2 Samuel 13:1)

You may say, "Yes, but this is surely describing their *faces*. They had pretty eyes and charming smiles. That is a far cry from noticing them from the neck down."

Read on (emphasis added):

> Leah's eyes were weak, but Rachel was *beautiful of form and face*. (Genesis 29:17)

> Now Joseph was *handsome in form and appearance*. (Genesis 39:6)

> [Mordecai] was bringing up Hadassah, that is Esther . . . the young woman had *a beautiful figure and was lovely to look at*. (Esther 2:7 ESV)

This is without a single reference to *Song of Solomon*!

The Bible acknowledges the objective good looks of shapely bodies (both men and women) and the attraction that we have to them. It does not portray this attraction as inherently evil. Certainly we must guard our eyes and our minds so that we do not cross the line from looking to lusting, but we should not deny the natural appreciation of the human body that God has created us with.

Now please do not misinterpret me! None of the people described in these biblical texts were naked. I am in no way endorsing pornography or suggesting that it is okay so long as we are only "looking, but not lusting." I am, however, trying to show that when a man notices a pretty woman, it does not make him the devil or a pervert.

Which brings up another point, and one that causes knots to form in my stomach as I think about it. I have two daughters. Some day, each of them is likely to be approached by a young man for marriage. Part of the reason he will be interested in my daughter is because he will think she has a beautiful figure and is lovely to look at. The very fact that he arrives at those conclusions proves he has been *looking* at her figure.

Admittedly, my first instinct will be to find my *Louisville Slugger*. But at the end of the day, this is utterly unrealistic. Not because all men are libido-driven hounds who cannot control their appetites, but because God has made us this way. Frankly, if a prospective husband does not find my daughter physically attractive, they shouldn't get married. Either he is a liar or he is going to make for a miserable husband. Certainly, if he crosses the line, I *will* go searching for the baseball bat. But anything behind the line is good and natural to humanity. Christians ought to know where the line is because we know the One who drew it.

Enjoying the appearance of your spouse's body is one of the pleasures of marriage. Make sure to take time to enjoy it.

> *The Bible acknowledges the objective good looks of shapely bodies (both men and women) and the attraction that we have to them.*

Stop & Discuss...

+ How was beauty treated in your home growing up? Was "looking good" encouraged, discouraged, or not discussed? How has that shaped your views today?
+ Describe something you find physically attractive about your spouse.

Cosmetics and Jewelry

Another issue confronting me as a father of girls is the propriety of jewelry, make-up, perfume, stylish clothes, and the like. My oldest daughter is sixteen, but her interest in these things began a long time ago. It caused me to ask, *Does the Bible speak to these things?* Yes it does.

Through the prophet Ezekiel, God spoke of Israel as His wife. When he first found her, she was a mess (16:4). She was alone and helpless, having been tossed into a field and left for dead (v5). God revived and sustained her (v6). Then, in a statement pertinent to our discussion, He said,

> "You grew up, became tall and *reached the age for fine ornaments*" (v7, emphasis mine).

According to God Himself, there is an appropriate age when a girl becomes ready to embellish her womanly features.

We will consider those embellishments shortly, but first I want to draw your attention to another thing God said in verse 7: "Your breasts were formed and your hair had grown." The man noticed the breasts of this young woman who attracted him. That husband, remember, is God. So God noticed the expanding bosom of a girl, and He found it attractive. This was not a sin for God, nor is it a sin for a man unless, of course, it gives way to lust. We will describe lust more extensively in our consideration of purity, but for now we should note that it is possible for a man to notice a woman's chest and not be sinning in the process.

Back to the embellishments. Lest we think that the "feminine decorations" were for the sole purpose of attracting a husband, the text goes on to describe what God did for His bride *after* they were married. He said,

> "I adorned you with ornaments, put bracelets on your hands, and a necklace around your neck. I also put a ring in your nostril, earrings in your ears and a beautiful crown on your head. Thus you were adorned with gold and silver, and your dress was of fine linen, silk and embroidered cloth. You ate fine flour, honey and oil; so you were exceedingly beautiful and advanced to royalty. Then your fame went forth among the nations on account of your beauty, for it was perfect because of My splendor which I bestowed on you," declares the Lord GOD. (Ezekiel 16:11-14)

This is how God treated His wife—He gave her bracelets, necklaces, nose rings, earrings, and a crown.

It was the good stuff, too, made of gold and silver. He bought her fancy dresses made out of expensive fabric. He also provided delectable food to eat. All of these things contributed to her exceeding beauty and popularity.

Husband, strive to be like God in this. Adorn your wife with ornaments and jewelry as He did. Personal decorations are not evil, nor do they make you worldly and materialistic. Beauty is part of God's creation. Hairstyling, rings, necklaces, perfume, nail polish, and all the rest are appropriate accessories to the feminine appearance.

Yes, there are passages in the New Testament which at first glance seem to downplay (if not outright deny) the place of ornamental decorations on women. The two most important are 1 Timothy 2:9-10 and 1 Peter 3:1-6. However, I am convinced that neither Peter nor Paul absolutely condemned the use of jewelry, braided hair, or fine clothes. Rather, they established a hierarchy of attractiveness for women. Number One on the list is her noble, respectful, submissive character and conduct. This is vastly more important than dressing to the nines and having a keen sense of fashion. However, assuming that a woman is pursuing this godly disposition on the inside, it is also natural to her gender to display her God-given beauty on the outside.

As with any good thing, the danger exists of making an idol out of a woman's looks. However, we must not let the *potential* of evil eliminate the *actual* enjoyment of the good. The bottom line is this: Buy things for your wife that communicate to her (and to those who see her) that she is your crown and glory (Prov. 12:4; 1 Cor. 11:7). And tell her *often* of her beauty, inside and out.

Stop & Discuss...

+ Wife, tell him how it makes you feel to know that he finds you physically attractive.
+ Wife, what is the correct biblical balance between being obsessed with appearances, clothes, jewelry, etc. and desiring to look beautiful and feminine?
+ Husband, what colors does she think look best on her? What kinds of clothing does she think fit her well? Does she prefer gold or silver? Big earrings or small? Tell her your thoughts and let her judge your accuracy.
+ Wife, what was the last gift of jewelry or clothing he gave you? How can be bless you in the future?

Sexual Pleasure

Of course, one cannot contemplate pleasure in marriage without considering sex. In many ways, it is *the* defining act of marriage and the culmination of all the other pleasures of the marital relationship. The topic deserves its own chapter, and so I will hold most of my comments until we get to it. However, I want to go this far for the moment and say that Christians need to guard against two extremes when discussing sexuality.

On one side is the profane, disgraceful, animalistic view held by the current American culture. We live among "experts" who give advice about "hooking up" with a co-worker at the office Christmas party and the potential benefits and pitfalls of spending the night with a colleague or boss. Such advice is shamelessly posted on the homepage of *Yahoo!* and *FOX News*. The only boundaries for the contemporary man or woman are the limits of their own desires. (Even those can be relaxed a bit after a drink or two). *Any man or woman, with any man or woman, anywhere, anytime* is our nation's view of sexuality. It's not a sacred thing, it's not a private thing, it's not an exclusive thing. It's just a thing.

The other side considers sex to be secret and taboo. We shouldn't talk about it as though we really do it or like it. This position takes God's beautiful creation, puts a blanket over it, and hides it in the attic where hopefully no one will find it.

The Bible is not even a little bit shy about discussing sexuality. When God condemned Israel for serving other gods, He unashamedly called her a whore who lifted up her skirt for every man who walked by. When He portrayed the great idol of materialism that consumed the unbelieving heart, He called her "Babylon the Great Prostitute." This is sexuality in its sinful, perverse form, which God conveyed uncensored.

The Scripture is equally unashamed to describe married sexuality as it is and should be. Solomon commanded his son to delight in his wife's breasts.

(Can you imagine your father talking to you about the allure of breasts?) The apostle Paul instructed husbands and wives to have sex frequently and consistently. If that were not enough, God devoted an entire book of the Bible to the physical, bodily, sexual ecstasy of marriage. Yes the same Spirit of God who inspired *Romans* also inspired *The Song of Solomon.*

> *In many ways, sex is the defining act of marriage and culmination of all the other pleasures of the marital relationship.*

Therefore, a wife who expresses pleasure in having sex with her husband is no more sinful than a wife who expresses joy in playing with her children. Both are blessings of God to be enjoyed for His glory and her delight.

We must take care not to fall off either side of the horse. We should not think of sexuality in crude, vulgar, or obscene ways, nor should we be embarrassed and sheepish about this generous gift from our Maker, a gift to be opened and celebrated without reservation.

> *God devoted an entire book of the Bible to the physical, bodily, sexual ecstasy of marriage.*

Stop & Discuss...

+ Have your views of sex been influenced by a depraved culture? Discuss any areas that you need to rethink in your marriage.
+ Are you prudish and reserved about your own sexual desires? Does it feel dirty? If so, why?
+ How open were your parents about their sexual relationship? Was sex more celebrated or taboo in your home growing up? How would you like it to be in your home with your kids?

God's Blessing on Our Sexual Pleasure

God encourages every husband to romance his wife —to kiss her, to touch her, to delight in her body. But this is not just a man's game. The same level of pleasure ought to be experienced by every wife. Affectionate, bodily, sexual joy is to be shared equally between a man and woman. Without a doubt there are differences, but they are matters of *how*, not *what*. Both partners are expected to find marriage to be an ocean of blessedness. God is pleased when a husband and wife sit next to each other on the porch, sip a cup of coffee, and share a chuckle at a silly squirrel's erratic behavior. He smiles when a man and wife flirt with each other through messages and email. He nods with affirmation when a guy runs his eyes up and down his wife's barely covered body on her way to the shower (and when he follows her in to watch). And He grants His hearty approval whenever a woman approaches her husband in order to enjoy the sexual ecstasy of making love. He made it, after all, right down to our most sensual body parts with their elated responses to the stimulations of touch. God is pleased when His children are sexually pleased.

Again, let's go back to the beginning. The summary statement made when God first instituted marriage, and the last word spoken before sin entered the picture, was that "the man and his wife were both naked and were not ashamed" (Gen. 2:25). Adam stood before Eve, and Eve before Adam, and neither of them gave a second thought to the fact that they were not wearing any clothes. It seemed right and natural. They liked looking at each other. They felt no humiliation, no disgrace, no hesitancy whatsoever at walking around the world, in front of God and all His creatures, buck-naked. It was good.

After they disobeyed, however, their free spirit went away, and they hid themselves as God drew near (Gen. 3:8). Previously, they were exposed. Now, they *felt* exposed. They couldn't stand it. They had to find something to cover their naked bodies. This was the physical response to the shame they felt in their soul. They knew they had sinned against God. Now more than anything they desired to hide that sin.

For Christians, the curse of sin has been reversed. Its shame and reproach have been laid on Another. We have no reason to fear when God draws near. This ought to free us to be naked and unashamed with each other again.

I am not suggesting that public nudity is, or ever was, allowed. Remember, Adam and Eve were the only human beings on the planet when they walked around in the buff. Whether God would have wanted them to remain disrobed in the presence of other men and women is a subject for another time. What I *am* suggesting, however, is that there should be no hesitance for a Christian man or woman to take off their clothes in front of their spouse.

Several issues may prevent this shamelessness and freedom. The most common are poor body image, guilt for sexual sins, and past sexual abuse.

If your spouse is ashamed of their body, you need to reassure them of your acceptance and attraction. This is all the more important in a culture with airbrushed supermodels and millions spent on cosmetic adjustments. On the other hand, the one who feels physically inadequate must be careful not to selfishly rob their spouse of joy and intimacy by withholding sex because of his or her self-perception.

When dealing with guilt for previous sexual sins, we must allow the gospel to speak into the bedroom and wipe away all of the stains. *All* of our wickedness has been swallowed up in the sea of forgiveness, even the perverse ones. Let them stay there forever. Enjoy your new, pure sex life in Christ.

Sexual abuse is an entirely different category. Healing usually requires the assistance of pastoral counsel. Compounding the problem is the fact that most sexual abuse victims resist admitting that it happened, or they try to minimize it and continue surviving. They eventually pull back from relational and physical intimacy.

If you have experienced any form of abuse—from someone lewdly exposing himself/herself to you, to inappropriate touching, to molestation, to rape—I cannot say it strongly enough, *talk to someone about it!* Joy and intimacy in life and marriage depend upon your getting help. Do not pretend that it did not happen or that it is no big deal. It *is* a big deal, for yourself and for your marriage.

Inhibition is the great pleasure-killer of sexual passion, and shyness about being naked together is a major inhibition. There should be no place where you are more comfortable and at ease than being undressed in full view of your mate. If you experience sexual difficultly or embarrassment in your marriage, please talk to your pastor about it.

Again, there is much more to come in the sex chapter, but for now, discuss the following questions.

Stop & Discuss...

+ Do you know any couples who seem to really enjoy marriage? How does it show?
+ Do you know couples who seem to have little or no joy in their marriage? How does that show?
+ Are you able to be naked and unashamed in front of each other in mind, soul, and body? Is this something you should talk about it with your pastor or a mentor couple?
+ Is there sexual sin in your past that is getting in the way of your sexual present?
+ Again, I cannot say it strongly enough: If either of you are victims of any sexual abuse (whether apparently minor or major) it is absolutely imperative that you discuss it with a pastoral counselor.

For His glory and our delight . . .

5

Purity

Sex That Belongs to You

As I said, sex is God's idea. He created it, He blessed it, He wants us to do it. There is nothing in the world more natural than for people to delight in sex, including all of its sights, sounds, scents, and sensations.

However, being *natural* does not make a thing *right*. For example, it is natural for a person to delight in ice cream. In this case, I am the most natural lover you could ever hope to meet. I love ice cream. It does not last long in my house because I consume it like I breathe air. Now, when I reach into *my* freezer, in *my* kitchen, and pop the lid off a carton of ice cream that *I own*, I am simply delighting in the good gift of God. I am eating *my* ice cream to the glory of God. (Isn't He a generous God?) However, if I break open a carton at the local grocery store, I am not glorifying God, I am sinning against Him. Eating ice cream is not sinful, eating *that* ice cream is. It is not mine to eat. It belongs to someone else. In the same way, sex is a wonderful way to bring glory to God (can I get another *Amen*?) when it is with your spouse. But between two people who are not married, it is sin, not because it is sex, but because it is "sex that doesn't belong to you."

Two Kinds of Sexual Sin

Sexual sin occurs in two locations: the head and the bed. Consider King David's sin with Bathsheba:

> In the spring of the year, the time when kings go out to battle, David sent Joab, and his servants with him, and all Israel. And they ravaged the Ammonites and besieged Rabbah. But David remained at Jerusalem. It happened, late one afternoon, when David arose from his couch and was walking on the roof of the king's house, that he saw from the roof a woman bathing; and the woman was very beautiful. And David sent and inquired about the woman. And one said, "Is not this Bathsheba, the daughter of Eliam, the wife of Uriah the Hittite?" So David sent messengers and took her, and she came to him, and he lay with her. (2 Samuel 11:1-4 ESV)

In this account, we find the great Israeli king taking an evening walk on the balcony of his palace, no doubt a common way for him to relax and think. As he stretched his legs and maybe sipped a cup of coffee while composing the next lyric to one of his psalms, his eyes scanned the horizon of his nation until they landed on a stunningly beautiful woman. Taking a bath. Naked.

Up to this point, David had not sinned in his head or his bed. As far as the text reveals, this was not a voyeuristic stroll on the rooftop. He had not planned this encounter. Nor was it his fault that Bathsheba was beautiful or naked. He simply happened onto this situation. Had he turned from looking at her and forbade his mind from thinking about what he saw, he could have avoided sin altogether. But he not only thought about her, he sent his servants to get her so that he could have sex with her. He ate ice cream that didn't belong to him.

Why did David do it? The Bible explains how sin works:

> But each person is tempted when he is lured and enticed by his own desire. Then desire when it has conceived gives birth to sin, and sin when it is fully grown brings forth death. (James 1:14-15 ESV)

The main clause of verse 14 is, *each is tempted.* Some English translations add "when" here, but James is really describing *how* a person is tempted. A man (or woman) is tempted "by his own desire," (Gr. *epithumeo*) an intense yearning for something. We all have powerful internal lusts which carry the potential for great sin.

For most men and many women, sexual desire is set to *maximum intensity* by default. You need to understand just how tenacious a sexual appetite can be. It has caused national wars and individual murders. It has destroyed marriages through adultery, pornography, and divorce. Even relationships that stay together can be severely crippled by its effects. (Its power can also drive a vibrant, loyal, passionate marriage. But since I am discussing sin here, we must focus on the dark side of the force.)

We should notice something else about temptation. James says that these lusts (literally) "bait us" and "drag us along" like a fish is lured to a worm. He means that if we see a desired object, we can be drawn to it with seemingly irresistible force. As the enticement grows, our desires seize control and seduce us. Eventually, the lust becomes pregnant and gives birth to sin, which grows up to death.

In order to avoid sin, we must kill the lust while it is still in the womb. We must eliminate it before the enticement takes control. In other words, when a desire is aroused, we must overcome it or destroy it before it has a chance to intensify, just as a fish must turn away from the worm to avoid being hooked. When David sees the captivating, naked Bathsheba, he must do something immediately which will put out the spark while it is still a flicker.

Sex is a wonderful way to bring glory to God when it is with your spouse. But when it occurs between two people who are not married, it is sin, not because it is sex, but because it is "sex that doesn't belong to you."

The Heart of the Matter

Before we discuss ways to resist sexual temptation, I want to consider a related statement of Jesus which I believe is often misunderstood:

> But I say to you that everyone who looks at a woman with lust for her has already committed adultery with her in his heart. (Matthew 5:28)

At first-glance, this text seems to mean something like, "Even if you do not have sex with a woman, if you think about having sex with her you are committing adultery in your head. Mind sex is just as sinful as body sex." Although I whole-heartedly agree with that affirmation, I do not think that that was our Lord's primary point. If we look closely at the wording, we see a slightly different assertion.

Though admittedly awkward in English, the statement literally reads something like this:

> The one who looks at a woman for the purpose of intensely desiring her already "adulterized" her in his heart.

Read it again and emphasize the word *already*. What has already happened? What is the result? The man has already committed adultery in his heart, and now he intensely desires her. Do you see the emphasis? His burning sexual craving for her exists because he has *already*, sometime in the past, maybe just seconds ago, had sex with her in his heart. Now he cannot get her out of his mind. He wants her in his bed, a yearning that would not be there if he had stopped short of having her in his head.

David committed adultery with Bathsheba first in his heart, then the pining grew until he could no longer remain ungratified. At that point, he sent for her. If, when he saw her, he had not gone through with the sexual act in his mind, or if he had quickly turned to desire something else, he would not have been carried away with lust. If you can prevent the sinful act from taking place in your heart, you can avoid the controlling desire that follows.

> *As you can see, our temptations are driven by strong desires. For most men and many women, sexual desire is set to "maximum intensity" by default. You need to understand just how tenacious a sexual appetite can be.*

Stop & Discuss...

+ Discuss how strong the sexual desire of most men and many women is. Discuss how strong each of your sexual desires are.
+ Describe the difference between sex that pleases God and sex that displeases Him.
+ Have you ever known a marriage in which adultery occurred? How did it impact the marriage? How could it have been prevented?
+ According to this section, what bodily organ is the source of our sexual sins? (Hint: it's not the genitals.)

Lust Protection—General Defense

How do we keep lust from growing into a formidable foe? How do we avert the adultery of the heart? First, we build a basic wall of defense by maintaining the Spiritual disciplines. We must renew our minds (Rom. 12:1-2). We must set our minds on things above (Col. 3:2). We must study God's Word, pray, fellowship regularly with other believers, and so on. We must develop a passion for righteousness, a love for what is good and a hatred for what is evil. We must ask the Lord to purify our heart and to grant us noble, Christ-honoring passions and desires. This is really what Jesus was getting at with the verses that follow His statement about looking on a woman with lust:

> If your right eye causes you to sin, tear it out and throw it away. For it is better that you lose one of your members than that your whole body be thrown into hell. And if your right hand causes you to sin, cut it off and throw it away. For it is better that you lose one of your members than that your whole body go into hell. (Matthew 5:29-30 ESV)

We read this and immediately think that eliminating sin calls for drastic measures. It sounds like Jesus is saying, "If you struggle with sexual lust, cut out your eyes so you cannot see." And we sincerely hope He is using hyperbole because we are not interested in amputating any part of our body. However, if Jesus is truly suggesting that we remove the body part doing the sin, then with respect to sexual lust neither the eye nor the hand will suffice. A man is perfectly capable of wanting and having sex without either of these. (Does a man need to see or touch a woman to fantasize about her?) The pertinent body part is a little lower.

But to think about body parts is to miss Jesus' point. The key player is neither the eye, nor the hand, nor the genitals. It is the heart:

> For *out of the heart* come evil thoughts, murder, adultery, sexual immorality, theft, false witness, slander (Matt. 15:19 ESV, emphasis added).

The way to eliminate sinful lust is to cut out your sinful heart. Not the organ that pumps blood, but the internal soul and will. In other words, purity comes not from external restraint, or even from the Law of God, but from internal transformation. We need a heart transplant, a new desire to please God.

Everyone who genuinely believes the gospel of Jesus Christ has received a new heart. It is one of the great blessings of the New Covenant (Ezek. 36:26-27). This means that a true Christian has both the desire and the ability to obey God. If you are not sure about the gospel, or about the sincerity of your faith, I urge you to drop everything else and study the Scripture until you are sure. Seek counsel from a wise pastor or Christian friend about what true saving faith is because you need the power of God's Spirit to help you remain faithful and pure in your marriage. Only believers have the Holy Spirit.

Yet *having* the new heart is not enough. We all need to perform the proper exercises (the Spiritual disciplines mentioned earlier) that will strengthen it in purity and goodness. The more our heart longs to show love to Christ, the less it will long for evil pursuits.

Lust Protection—Specific Defense

Second, we need to learn from Joseph and run from temptation (Gen. 39:6f). When Potiphar's wife tried to seduce him, he ran out of the house not even stopping to pick up the shirt she had ripped off of him. That was a good technique for remaining pure.

When David saw Bathsheba, he should have immediately turned away from the beautiful-yet-potentially-sinful sight before him. Again, accidentally finding himself staring at the disrobed woman was not his sin. It's what he did next that led to adultery.

There is one more thing to consider. Leaving the roof would have prevented David from sinning in his bed, but not necessarily in his head. Now that his sexual desire was aroused, what was he to do with it? He could have taken a cold shower or hit the weight room. But he also had a way, a God-given way, mind you, to satisfy those desires righteously. He could have sexually pursued his wife (or in his case, wives).

In 1 Corinthians 7, the apostle Paul gives very practical instructions for marriage sexuality:

> But because of immoralities, each man is to have his own wife, and each woman is to have her own husband. The husband must fulfill his duty to his wife, and likewise also the wife to her husband. The wife does not have authority over her own body, but the husband does; and likewise also the husband does not have authority over his own body, but the wife does. Stop depriving one another, except by agreement for a time, so that you may devote yourselves to prayer, and come together again so that Satan will not tempt you because of your lack of self-control. (1 Corinthians 7:2-5)

While not the stuff of a best-selling romantic novel, many real life marriages would be saved or greatly improved if the commands of this text were consistently obeyed.

The instruction is quite clear. Every spouse is obligated to "be there" for his or her partner when sexual passions are aroused. It is one of the divine purposes of marriage. On your wedding day, you handed over all sexual rights to your mate. Your, "I do," meant, "I will, whenever you want." Your body is no longer yours to keep, it belongs to your spouse. So if you avoid sex, you're basically stealing.

The only reason a married couple should abstain from consistent lovemaking is for a special period of prayer. But even that is not a good enough reason to go without for very long. The apostle acknowledges that our urges are too strong and influential to be left unfulfilled for any extended amount of time. Mark it well, the Bible commands regular, frequent sex in your marriage to help you both remain sexually pure.

Here's how it works in the real world: Husband, when confronted with a situation which stirs your sexual appetite, you are not necessarily required to hate the desire, or ignore it, or replace it with another desire. Instead, you may turn to your wife. If she desires to please her Lord, she will happily be your fulfillment. She will see it as a means of humbly serving you in your efforts to resist lustful temptations. This goes both ways. If you neglect your wife's sexual needs, you are sinning against her. You must not prevent her from enjoying what God has generously provided to her. You must pursue a steady, sexually charged relationship with her. You are both obligated to do your erotic duty for the other. (Awful, isn't it? Like being required to eat ice cream every day.)

King Solomon taught the same thing as Paul, only more poetically, when he wrote,

> Let your fountain be blessed, and rejoice in the wife of your youth, a lovely deer, a graceful doe. Let her breasts fill you at all times with delight; be intoxicated always in her love. (Proverbs 5:18-19 ESV)

First, I must say that anyone who considers the Bible to be stiff, clinical, and restrictive about sex simply has not read it. Sex within marriage is to be rigorously and habitually delighted in. And the Spirit-inspired writers do not hesitate to tell it like it is. Second, Solomon knew that men like breasts. He knew that God created this desire, and he was not embarrassed to acknowledge it. Why should he be? Nor was he intimidated by the subject. He was happy to admit to his son that breasts are a source of wonderful delight, and that he should indulge himself without restraint, even to the point of virtual breast-drunkenness, so long as he is only drinking wine from his own wine cellar. Men are not to be enchanted by every woman's breasts, only *his* woman's breasts.

The greater context of Proverbs 5 deals with avoiding the temptress. Solomon knew that adultery is a path leading straight to the City of Destruction. He desperately wanted his son to stay off that path. The way to steer clear of the danger zone was to find great sexual satisfaction in his wife because a man who is happy in his bed at home (which he *should* be in) is not likely to seek happiness in the bed of another home (which he *should not* be in). Or as my wife likes to say, "If I feed him well at home, he won't want to eat out." Again, marriage is one of God's provisions for purity and for avoiding the allurement of sexual sin.

Once more I should qualify that what is true for the husband is true for the wife. Women have lusts too and are just as capable of adultery as men. A wife must delight in her husband's body and exclusively seek to gratify her desires with him. God has graciously provided this way (but only this one way) for her to experience physical, affectionate bliss.

Of course, this requires a willing and capable participant. Too often today, men delight themselves in the surgically created breasts of forbidden cyber women and have little desire for their wife. They have eaten synthetically produced sweeteners for so long, they have lost their taste for real sugar. After spending so much time in the world of fantasy, real life seems dull and unsatisfactory. They refuse to engage in sexual activities with their wife (or it becomes irregular, boring, and perfunctory) and thereby take away her means of purity and physical pleasure. His impurity becomes the cause of her impurity. When one loses, they both lose. This is not how God intends marriage to be.

> *Your, "I do," meant, "I will, whenever you want."*

To put this very practically, husband let me encourage you to proceed like this (wife, adjust as necessary): When you are standing in a Walmart checkout line, and you see a magazine cover displaying a gorgeous, scantily clad woman surrounded by stimulating titles like "95 Ways to Make Him Scream Using *Jello* and a Turkey Baster," or you are the victim of a surprise-attack *Victoria's Secret* commercial, or your favorite Christian website contains an article on the increasingly promiscuous sexual practices of young

American women, or the car in front of you is covered with provocative bumper stickers, or you are up on your roof cleaning the gutters when the teenaged girl next door decides to work on her tan in the backyard, or you hear someone like me going on and on about the delights and joys and thrills of sexual ecstasy, rather than suppressing or denying or being ashamed of your natural, God-given reactions to those kinds of stimuli, use them as the impetus to pursue your spouse. Instead of putting the mental moves on a woman who lives in your dreams, put the physical moves on the woman who lives in your house. That is one of the reasons God gave her to you.

I can tell you from first-hand experience that when I aggressively pursue my wife sexually—pondering her body, daydreaming about what we might do together, longing to be with her, planning opportunities to realize these fantasies—my desire for other women (real or imagined) is akin to my affection for cats. I can also tell you from years of marriage counseling that when a couple stops pursuing each other sexually, big troubles lie ahead.

> *Mark it well, the Bible commands regular, frequent sex in your marriage for the purpose of avoiding temptation. This is how being married will help you both remain sexually pure.*

To summarize, when either of you is tempted sexually, you have two options for dealing with it:

1. Turn your mind to something else altogether.

2. Turn your sexual desire toward your spouse and seek fulfillment there.

When I discuss this in pre-marital counseling, the couples usually find it hard to believe that I even need to bring it up. It seems absurd to those struggling to keep their hands off of each other that God has to *command* married couples to have sex. Sadly, for many marriages there is nothing absurd about it. If you do not take this seriously, one or both of you will become frustrated, dissatisfied, and tempted to sin. I talk to spouses all the time, both men and women, who feel robbed and unloved because their partner refuses them sexually. They all started out thinking their love would be a passionate ocean, but it has become more like a shriveling puddle. Don't become a shriveling puddle!

Stop & Discuss...

+ How does a person develop a desire for righteousness? How does this help fight lust?
+ Do you understand how and why lust is a sin of the mind, not the body? Explain.
+ On your wedding day, you each signed over the deed to your body to the other. Do you realize the implications of this? Are you serving each other sexually whenever and as often as the other desires? Discuss.
+ Do you understand that all fantasizing about and wishing to be sexually involved with anyone other than your spouse is sin? (This includes people in romance novels, chick flicks, and porn.)
+ Wife, you need to sexually feed your husband well at home. Husband, you must feed only at home and feed often. Are you both doing your part?

6

Providence

The fourth purpose for marriage is *providence*. (This is the fourth "P." Can you name the first three?)

Providence derives from Latin and connotes foresight or concerned awareness of what is coming. God exercises providence over His creation as He cares for, guides, rules, protects, and organizes the world and all of its inhabitants. Thus, usually we regard providence as an attribute of God rather than of man. Yet mankind is given a significant role to play in God's cosmic care. Our responsibilities are explained in the beginning, when God created everything (including marriage):

Then God said, "Let Us make man in Our image, according to Our likeness; and let them rule over the fish of the sea and over the birds of the sky and over the cattle and over all the earth, and over every creeping thing that creeps on the earth." God created man in His own image, in the image of God He created him; male and female He created them. God blessed them; and God said to them, "Be fruitful and multiply and fill the earth, and subdue it; and rule over the fish of the sea and over the birds of the sky, and over every living thing that moves on the earth." (Genesis 1:26-28)

The Image of God

An important statement made repeatedly in this brief section is that men and women were created in the image of God. While there is some uncertainty about what *image of God* means because the Bible does not spell it out precisely, everyone agrees that it is of great consequence.

Whatever else may be intended, it includes the right and responsibility for humans to rule:

Let us make man in Our image . . . and *let them rule over* the fish of the sea. (v26, emphasis mine)

Rule (Heb. *radah*) is used to describe:

+ The authority of a master over his slave (Lev. 25:43, 46)

+ Solomon's kingdom which extended over great distances (1 Kings 4:24)

+ Solomon's commanders who managed his workers as they constructed the temple (1 Kings 5:16)

+ The reign of the Messiah from "sea to sea, and from the River to the ends of the earth" (Psa. 72:8)

That is the nature of the responsibility and authority granted to men and women.

In v28, another word is added—*subdue*. This Hebrew word (*kabash*) means "to bring into bondage." It is used:

+ Of Israel's capture and control of the promised land (Num. 32:22, 29; Josh. 18:1)

+ To describe all of the nations which David conquered (2 Sam. 8:11)

+ Of the sons and daughters of Israel being enslaved to their enemies (Neh. 5:4).

God expects mankind to be ruling and subduing His creation.

Another passage which summarizes the sovereignty of mankind is Psalm 8:

> What is man that You take thought of him, and the son of man that You care for him? Yet You have made him a little lower than God, and You crown him with glory and majesty! You make him to rule over the works of Your hands; You have put all things under his feet, all sheep and oxen, and also the beasts of the field, the birds of the heavens and the fish of the sea, whatever passes through the paths of the seas. (vv. 4-8)

The care and governance God has entrusted to us extends to fish of the sea, birds of the air, cattle, all the earth, every creeping thing (Gen. 1:26, 28), the works of God's hands, and all things (Psa. 8). That is a lot of responsibility!

Stop & Discuss...

+ Review: what does *providence* mean?
+ How does God exercise providence over His creation?
+ What role does mankind play in God's providence?
+ According to this study, what does it mean that humans are created in the image of God?
+ How do you rule and subdue? What does that look like in your life?
+ Can you guess how marriage includes the idea of providence?

That is the overview from Genesis 1. Genesis 2 explains specifically how God intends males and females to exercise this dominion. He had a structure in mind which has direct implications for your marriage.

God formed the male from the dust (v7) and placed him in the garden (v8) to cultivate [lit. *work*] it and keep [*take care of, guard*] it (v15). But God determined that it was not good for the male to do this by himself, so He decided to make a helper for him (v18). After examining all of the living creatures, it was obvious that none of them were adequate (v20). So God took a part of the man's body and manufactured a creature worthy of being his helper (v21f.). There was now a male and a female on the earth.

We should not lose sight of the purpose for which man was first created and for which woman was created after the man. *They were made to rule the earth.* God placed Adam in the garden to take care of it, and He gave Eve to Adam to help him in this work. Adam could not do it alone. Eve was his complement, his assistant ruler/worker. Together as vice-regents they would exercise the divine lordship over all that God had created. That means that *your* marriage has a part to play in God's providence over the world.

A Gardening Team

I have been placed in a garden. I have been given responsibility to teach the Word of God, to shepherd His sheep, and to lead the church in matters of faith and obedience. I must work that soil so that it produces fruit. I must guard it against predators, diseases, or drought. Husband, your vocation may be different, but whatever the field, you have the responsibility to cultivate and keep it for its own good and the glory of God.

Your wife is given to help you do it. She is the *gardener's assistant.* Lest we read into that term a false idea that an assistant is nothing more than a warm body who pushes pencils and retrieves coffee, we should note that in marriage the assistant is equal in dignity, value, and purpose to the gardener. She is a partner, not a hired hand. However, she does not have her own garden. Her job is to help her husband tend the patch that God put *him* in.

Does this mean that a wife may not pursue anything that does not include being literally next to her husband's side with a hoe in hand? No, but it does mean that she should not pursue anything that takes her from his side *figuratively*. She is designed to complement her husband, completing him and filling in the empty places, so that he can be more fruitful in his labors. If she is so removed or otherwise occupied that she does not know whether he is growing pumpkins or beans, or if she needs GPS to find the garden, it is unlikely that she is fulfilling her role faithfully.

To be very practical and specific, you, husband, need to determine what God has called you to do in this world. You need to discern your talents, gifts, abilities, and interests, and get to work in subduing the portion of the earth that is under your influence. This includes your career, of course, but it also includes your roles in your family, church, community, etc.

Every man has several gardens for which he is responsible. His wife's calling is to help him reach his potential in each of them.

Genesis 2
*Man is given **responsibility** for the garden.*
*Woman is created to **help** the man.*

This will not necessarily look the same for every marriage because men need different kinds of help. Still, some needs are almost universal. For example, one of my gardens is my family. The Lord has graciously granted me stewardship over three children, and I am accountable for their maturity in Christ. I must teach them God's Word and to obey Jesus' commands. I must teach them how to avoid the pitfalls of life and stay on the straight path. I must prepare them to be influential in their own gardens (or those of their husbands, in the cases of my two daughters). Now, if I spent all of my time teaching my children, I would be neglecting my other gardens, such as the church. I am just as accountable to the Chief Shepherd for my instruction of His sheep as I am for my family. How am I going to produce good fruit in both gardens?

By myself, the task would be almost impossible. But because God has given me a wonderful helper, I have the prospect of being productive in multiple areas that God has assigned to me. I do some instructing of our children, but my wife does the majority of it. Because of her invaluable help, I am fulfilling my responsibility, and we have a fertile patch with tall plants and minimal weeds. She also assists my pastoral ministry in more ways than I can count. Together, we are exercising providential care over our family and the church. That is how God intended marriage to work.

This does not mean that women have to work exclusively at home. There was a time in our marriage when my wife stood by my side by going out to work and earning substantial income. Yet even when a wife works outside the home, she ought to be doing it as an intentional act of assistance to her husband, not as a fulfillment of her own career ambition for its own sake. She is called to help him, not merely defray the cost of their shared apartment while he goes his way and she goes hers. (He took a wife, not a roommate.) Together, they need to decide what she can do that will be the most helpful in making their gardens successful.

> *Marriages have a part to play in God's providence over the world.*

Proverbs 31 Woman

The model wife is the woman described in Proverbs 31:10-31. The opening statement acknowledges her prowess and rarity:

An excellent wife, who can find?

Good wives, it seems, do not grow on trees. If you find one, you have a treasure worth more than a large pile of money.

The *Proverbs 31 Woman* is a wife who truly knows how to be a helpmate to her husband. We must be careful to observe that she does not sit around the house dressed to the nines, sipping tea and eating bonbons while the governess performs all the wifely duties of the home. No, this girl is not afraid to get dirt under her fingernails. It is also clear that her labor is not confined to the four walls of her house. Still, everything she does is for the benefit of, and with a view toward, her husband and home.

Here are the verses with brief comment:

> An excellent wife, who can find? For her worth is far above jewels. (v10)

The word *excellent* is the word for strength, might, and honor. The LXX (Greek translation of the OT) describes her as "manly." This does not mean that an excellent wife should look and act like a man. But she does possess some of the character qualities usually associated with masculinity. A good wife has a measure of strength and nobility that makes her man feel proud and wealthier than a billionaire.

> The heart of her husband trusts in her, and he will have no lack of gain. (v11)

A sturdy, virtuous woman can be trusted and entrusted. She will do what is right. She will turn a profit from the responsibility given to her. Rather than shopping away what her husband brings in, the excellent wife will add to it.

> She does him good and not evil all the days of her life. (v12)

The husband of this woman never thinks, *What have I done by marrying this person? Will she destroy me and the kids? When she gets done, will we have anything left? Is it always going to be like this?* To the contrary, he rests his head on his pillow at night thankful to share a bed with such a model of decency and grace.

> She looks for wool and flax and works with her hands in delight. She is like merchant ships; she brings her food from afar. (v13-14)

This woman is not likely to make a career of hand-modeling because of the callouses and scars. Her hands are beautiful nonetheless because they provide such blessings to her family. She is not content to simply throw any old thing on the backs of her kids, nor does she serve frozen dinners night after night. She uses her resourcefulness to provide fine clothes and food for them.

> She rises also while it is still night and gives food to her household and portions to her maidens. (v16)

The sun does not beat her out in the morning. More important than sleep is providing a good breakfast for her family. A selfless devotion to her home is her highest priority.

"Portions" is, literally, *statutes* or *prescribed tasks* (LXX, *work*). She oversees her daughters and the other ladies in the home (cp. Titus 2: 5), making sure they learn to be diligent as well. Under her supervision, the home remains in good order.

> She considers a field and buys it; from her earnings she plants a vineyard. (v16)

With a flair for investments, the excellent wife knows a good deal when she sees it, and she turns it into a valuable asset for the family. A modern day equivalent might be a woman who knows where to acquire underpriced items and resell them for a profit on eBay.

The husband of this woman rests his head on his pillow at night thankful to share a bed with such a model of decency and grace.

She girds herself with strength and makes her arms strong. (v17)

She finds time to hit the gym. In order to accomplish all her work, she disciplines herself to remain fit and capable of endurance. A sweaty workout is neither taboo nor neglected.

> She senses that her gain is good; her lamp does not go out at night. She stretches out her hands to the distaff, and her hands grasp the spindle. (v18-19)

Her Excellency holds an accurate assessment of her worth. She knows the benefit she provides her husband and children through her persistent exertion, and this knowledge spurs her on to greater industry. Not only does she start before the sun, she does not quit until long after it has retired for the evening. Whether she is cooking, cleaning, sewing, ironing, or planning, you are not likely to be awake without her being awake. And you can be sure she will be busy.

> She extends her hand to the poor, and she stretches out her hands to the needy. (v20)

Compassionate and tender toward those who are less fortunate, she holds out a helping hand or shares some of the profit from her labors with them.

> She is not afraid of the snow for her household, for all her household are clothed with scarlet. She makes [bed] coverings for herself; her clothing is fine linen and purple. (v21-22)

The excellent wife is prepared for the varying temperatures that come with the seasonal changes, manifesting a sense of style to go with her very practical diligence.

> Her husband is known in the gates, when he sits among the elders of the land. (v23)

With a wife like this, a man is able to apply himself to his work without being constantly preoccupied with the management of the home. Her dedication and responsible stewardship are a significant part of what makes him successful. As the saying goes, "Behind every good man is a good woman."

> She makes linen garments and sells them, and supplies belts to the tradesmen. (v24)

This lady understands the concepts of free market economy, supply and demand, and how to manufacture quality products.

> Strength and dignity are her clothing, and she smiles at the future. (v25)

When her husband thinks of his precious bride, it is not her fine dresses or fashionable shoes that linger in his mind, it is her distinguished, majestic character that he sees. She is not a woman who is easily distracted or dissuaded from reaching her objectives. She will not allow the fear of what lies ahead to control her now.

> She opens her mouth in wisdom, and the teaching of kindness is on her tongue. (v26)

Not only does she possess physical strength and entrepreneurial competence, this rare jewel is also smart and gracious. She does not act with pride because of her achievements. Instead, she transfers her aptitude to others so that they may also enjoy such delight. Even in this, her virtues are apparent as she gently instructs her students.

> She looks well to the ways of her household, and does not eat the bread of idleness. (v26)

Where does this exceptional woman focus her attention? Who is it all for? She expends her energy for the sake of one location—her home. She is not after her own career, nor is she seeking to make a name for herself. She does it all as a blessing to her husband and her children. They are the reason she refuses to be lazy or to spend her time on vain, slothful pastimes. She is not addicted to social media or infatuated with the latest twists of the new queen of pop. She has work to do for her man.

> *When her husband thinks of his precious bride, it is not her fine dresses or fashionable shoes that linger in his mind, it is her distinguished, majestic character that he sees.*

> Her children rise up and bless her; her husband also, and he praises her, saying: "Many daughters have done nobly, but you excel them all." (v28-29)

The profuse blessings she provides for her family do not go unnoticed. Her kids stand when she enters the room out of profound respect and appreciation. They love her and tell her so.

That goes double for her husband. Only a first-rate numbskull would fail to notice or express his gratitude for the bountiful, generous good she has done to him. He rightfully observes that no other woman is worthy to be compared to his gem. He is the most blessed of men, indeed.

> Charm is deceitful and beauty is vain, but a woman who fears the LORD, she shall be praised. Give her the product of her hands, and let her works praise her in the gates. (v30-31)

Wife, do not think that your shapely curves, pretty hair, or beautiful eyes are going to remain your only attractive features. As you please Christ by prospering and blessing your husband and children, you will become more lovely than any amount of cosmetic efforts can make you.

Imagine a world where men who know their places in it team up with women like that! God's creation would certainly be well taken care of if our marriages matched the biblical ideal.

Stop & Discuss...

+ The Bible does not sentence a wife to a "barefoot and pregnant" existence, nor does it condone her living as a housemate with her husband while pursuing her own agenda. Explain what I mean by that.
+ Specifically, how does a man exercise providence over the earth?
+ Husband, do you know your gardens? What are they?
+ How does a wife exercise providence over the earth?
+ Wife, how do you help your husband cultivate his gardens? Can you do more?
+ Husband, what impresses you about the Proverbs 31 wife?
+ Wife, why would a feminist consider the Proverbs 31 wife to be degraded? Do you?

The Question Every Wife Asks

Early in the Spirit-inspired love poem known as *Song of Solomon* there is an interchange that occurs almost daily in every married home. See if you can spot it:

Tell me, you whom my soul loves, where you pasture your flock, where you make it lie down at noon; for why should I be like one who veils herself beside the flocks of your companions?

If you do not know, O most beautiful among women, follow in the tracks of the flock, and pasture your young goats beside the shepherds' tents. (Song of Solomon 1:7-8 ESV)

Did you catch it? This is the poetic version of a wife asking, "How was work today?" Only something is amiss here because the man did not reply, "Fine," as he flips his thumb along the display of his smart phone.

In this love song, the lover wants to know about her husband's work. She is interested in his vocation. Furthermore, she refuses to be a mere bystander or casual acquaintance. She wants to have intimate knowledge of his skills and workplace. She is jealous of other women who know more details of his profession. She scorns the thought of being no more than a far off observer. She wants to know more about him and his daily labors than any other human being on the planet.

Wife take note—*every man wants to be respected by his wife*. Men were created to work, and we long for our wife to be the loudest cheerleader for our endeavors. We want to believe that she finds something attractive and fascinating about that to which we give so much of our time and energy. But we want more than just rah-rah and pompons. We yearn for a woman who shows sincere interest in, and admiration for, our work.

It seems that women too often resent their husband's devotion to a job. Now, I readily admit that some men seem to cherish their work more than their wife and thereby earn the resentment. But if a man keeps work in proper balance, his wife should appreciate his diligence. She should find his job a stimulus for affection. The skill, provision, and proficiency she observes in her man's work should have an arousing affect on her.

In the *Song*, the man responds by inviting his wife to go where the action is and see it for herself. He welcomes her to know what he does and how he does it. He is pleased with her interest.

Compare his response to the commonplace dialogue which will occur in thousands of homes across America this evening:

Wife: Hi, Honey, how was your day?

Husband: Fine.

Wife: (walking away) Dinner will be ready in 15 minutes.

Husband: Okay.

These few words communicate a lot. The husband hears the run-of-the-mill, ordinary, mostly meaningless greeting from his wife. It is not much different than just "Hi." Whether consciously or not, he does not find any good reason to think that she cares about his work. So, he responds abruptly and blandly with "Fine."

This is what she hears: *He doesn't want me to be involved in this part of his life, the part which consumes so much of him. He will talk to his buddies for hours about his job, but all I get is "Fine." It's always just fine.* So, she changes her attention and walks away.

Such indifference gives him further evidence that her initial inquiry was just a formality. *See how quickly she moves on. There's no follow-up question, no genuine desire to know. At least my buddies really want to know what I am doing and dealing with at the office.*

He says, "Okay" which tells her that she was right. He is content to talk to the guys about his job, while using her for cooking, cleaning, and sex. (Too bad the guys can't take care of those things, too!)

Both parties failed here. The wife needs to find more creative ways to inquire. "How was your day?" can become stale and routine. Although technically a question, it can be received as nothing more than a statement such as *Hey!* or *What's up?* And, of course, when someone asks, *What's up?* the expected response is, *Nothing much.* That is how our culture works. It is normal. However, marriage always has to beware of *normal* becoming lifeless and tired.

The wife needs to come up with different ways to ask the question. She should continually add to her understanding of his work. As she does, she can ask better, more informed questions. For example, in the morning she could ask something like, "Is there anything at work today that you are particularly concerned about or excited about? How can I specifically pray for you today?" Then, of course, she should give some thought and prayer to it. When he returns home, she can ask about it.

Again, standard phrases should be avoided. "How was your meeting?" is not as good as, "Tell me about your meeting with John. Did it go as you expected?" And definitely communicate that you prayed for that meeting specifically (assuming you did). Ponder what concerned your husband, why it concerned him, and how he handled the situation. This will help you ask intelligent questions in the future when similar meetings are planned.

Conversely, the husband should not assume that just because the language is traditional the intent is disingenuous. If this woman is the love of his life, part of his own flesh, his covenant partner for as long as they both shall live, then why would he *not* want to share the details of his work? He should desire to experience everything in life with his wife. This includes his work. There may be aspects of a job that another man can identify with more fully simply because he is a man, but this must not preclude you from allowing or (better) *inviting* your wife to participate in regular knowledge of your vocation.

> *Marriage always has to beware of normal becoming lifeless and tired.*

A man's hesitancy to discuss his job with his wife is not due to her inability to comprehend, but to his laziness and selfishness. Or, sometimes, because she really does not care. Either way, the marriage lacks a vital component for intimacy and unity.

Wife, make it part of your routine to learn about your husband's job. Convince him that you want to be part of it. Find non-routine ways to express it. Husband, tell her about it. Include her in your work. Allow her the privilege of participating in this important part of who you are.

Stop & Discuss...

+ Explain to each other how your mothers showed (or did not show) interest in your father's work.
+ Did your fathers seem excited to share their professional details with your mothers?
+ Wife, what can you do to increasingly appreciate the significance of your husband's vocation?
+ Husband, how will you maintain a desire to share this important aspect of your life with your wife?

Titus 2 Woman

Another important text for wives is the second chapter of Titus. The apostle Paul instructs as follows.

> Older women likewise are to be reverent in their behavior, not malicious gossips nor enslaved to much wine, teaching what is good, so that they may encourage the young women to love their husbands, to love their children [lit. *to be husband-loving, children-loving*], to be sensible, pure, workers at home [lit. *house-stewards*], kind, being subject to their own husbands, so that the word of God will not be dishonored. (2:3-5)

A wife should be a woman who loves her husband and her children (in that order). Adjectives such as trendy, fun, wealthy, funny, conversational, or popular are important to the world, but Christian women care more about honoring Christ through their devotion to their men and kids. Part of the "providential" responsibility given to women is that as they become older and wiser they should pass on their prudence to younger women, seeking to instill godly virtue in them. Wife, consider seeking a mature, godly mentor to learn the art and skill of blessing your husband.

A second noteworthy instruction is that young wives should be "workers at home," or, literally, "house-stewards." This is important both for husbands and wives to understand. A man is the head of his home. He is responsible for it. However, the wife is the steward of the home. She is to be delegated the authority to oversee the home as though she were its owner. The man grants control over domestic affairs to the woman. This means that the husband now places himself under the authority of the wife in day-to-day activities. It works out something like this. If the wife desires dinner to take place at 5:30 p.m., the man complies cheerfully. If the wife wants to paint the guest bathroom green, the husband agrees, and helps her do it. The home is her domain. *Domain* derives from the Latin for 'lord' (*dominus*). She is the lord of the home or, as they used to say it, the "mistress of the house."

This does not mean that in the final analysis the wife rules over the husband in the home. He is still the king of his castle. However, he gives the every day governance to her. For example, as the steward of my house, meals come under the responsibility of my wife. I do not (usually) decide what we have for breakfast or lunch or dinner. What my wife cooks, I eat. Without complaint. However, as the head of the home, I am concerned with the broad principles of our meal planning. If my wife were to regularly spend more than the budgeted amount on groceries, thereby putting us into financial danger, I would then intervene to see what can be done to curb these expenditures. At that point, she would submit to me regarding our eating. Or I may ask her to keep the menu on the healthy side of things so that the family can try to avoid the perils of having too much fat in our diets. Or I might want her to reserve elaborate, fancy dinners for special occasions such as holidays or when we have guests, so that those times are and remain special. But beyond these kinds of foundational desires, my wife rules the roost, and I do as I am told.

Summary

By God's design, a husband needs a helper, and a wife needs to help him. To ignore or circumvent this pattern is like trying to make a car go without wheels and wheels go without a car. It is possible, but not nearly as effective. On the other hand, when a marriage operates like it is supposed to, the richest, most productive, most satisfying partnership imaginable is created and maintained, to the glory of God and the good of His world.

Stop & Discuss...

+ Wife, do you have a mature godly mentor who can help you grow in your love for, and devotion to, your husband and home?
+ How do things work in your home? Who does what around the house? How are the chores divided up? Should you make any changes?
+ Husband, do you know your need for a helper? Explain it to her.
+ Wife, do you know your need to help? Explain it to him.
+ Are you each doing your part to rule and subdue the earth?

7

Parenting

Looking back again to the original creation of the man and the woman, we find that they were designed to "be fruitful and multiply, and fill the earth" (Gen. 1:28). Adam and Eve would be the root of an enormous family tree covering the earth with humanity. After all, the world is a big place; if men and women were expected to rule over and subdue it, it would take a bunch of them.

This design feature was not unique to pristine, pre-fall humanity. That is, nothing about the plan changed after Adam and Eve plunged into sin. We know this because after God judged the world in the flood, He gave the same command to the eight people who were spared. God wanted Noah, his sons, and their wives to "populate the earth abundantly and multiply in it" (Gen. 9:7).

In procreating, we demonstrate more of what it means to be made in the image of God. He created the heavens and the earth, then He created life in the man and the woman, then He gave *them* the ability to create life by having children. God multiplied plants and animals all over the earth, but He gave mankind the authority to multiply people all over the earth. What an awesome responsibility and privilege!

We must be careful not to separate this purpose from the others. For decades, our culture has been taught that we are the descendants of animals, and in virtually every way we act like we believe it. Reproduction is no exception. When it comes to mating, animals are largely indiscriminate and promiscuous. One male dog may be responsible for impregnating the mothers of all the neighborhood puppies within five blocks. And that is fine *for dogs*! For humanity, however, God has instructed a man to leave his father's household and begin his own by cleaving to a wife. It is in that (and only that!) united, committed, exclusive, permanent relationship that children are intended to be born.

The divine design is not merely that we multiply like rabbits, but that we nurture those whom we bring into the world. We are to *rear* children, not just *breed* them. The apostle Paul assumes this when he writes to the Christians in Ephesus:

> Children, obey your parents in the Lord, for this is right. Honor your father and mother (which is the first commandment with a promise), so that it may be well with you, and that you may live long on the

earth. Fathers, do not provoke your children to anger,
but bring them up in the discipline and instruction of
the Lord. (Ephesians 6:1-4)

Children are given to parents and are obligated to
submit to their authority. This cannot happen without
adults who properly assume the parental role. Fathers
are expressly commanded to teach their children to love
and obey the Lord Jesus Christ, and to do so in a way
that does not provoke wrath in them.

We see this assumption throughout the Scriptures.
Dad and mom are the presupposed teachers of the child
when Solomon writes, "Hear, my son, your father's
instruction, and do not forsake your mother's
teaching" (Prov. 1:8). And the author of Hebrews
compares the way that the heavenly Father trains His
sons to that of human fathers: "It is for discipline that
you endure; God deals with you as with sons; for what
son is there whom his father does not discipline?" (Heb.
12:7). Children are supposed to be born to a husband
and wife who will remain together ("cleave") and guide
them toward godliness.

"Behold, children are a heritage from the LORD, the
fruit of the womb a reward," says the psalmist (Psa.
127:3 ESV). Those who love the Lord ought to view
them as such. They are not accidents, inconveniences,
necessary evils, tolerable nuisances, or merely the
future bearers of our grandchildren. They are blessings
from God. Parents who consider their children a chore,
or pests who constantly get in the way of their lives,
must repent of their sin and start regarding them as
precious gifts from their Creator.

As with every aspect of life, the ability to have children lies ultimately in the sovereign will of God. In some cases He withholds this privilege, but in most cases He grants it. When a man and woman enter into the marriage covenant, they ought to come assuming, expecting, and desiring to enjoy the experience of having kids.

I do not believe that the Scripture requires a specific number of children, much less that couples have as many children as possible. Nor are there commands regarding when and how often. As with all of life, wisdom and good stewardship principles must be applied to having children.

Stop & Discuss...

[This section is brief because it's a marriage book, not a parenting book. But it will still be helpful to discuss these questions.]

+ If you have young kids at home, you need to be unified on what the Bible says about discipline and on how you implement it. Are you together?

+ Are you together on how to educate them, what activities they will be involved in (sports, arts, youth group, etc.), and similar things?

+ The goal is not to raise well-educated, upstanding American citizens, but to raise godly adults who love Christ. What's the difference and how will you accomplish this?

+ How will you keep your marriage as a higher passion and priority than your children?

+ If your kids are older, are you a team in how you relate to them, encourage them, and love them?

8

The Only Marriage Problem

It's Not Communication

Read the books, go to the conferences, listen to the "experts" and you may come away thinking that if couples could just learn to communicate more effectively, their marital difficulties would vanish into thin air. We just need to become better listeners, choose gentler terms, and repeat back what was said to ensure that we are "hearing each other correctly." Condemning tones and critical barbs must go, along with defensiveness, stonewalling, or giving the "silent treatment." Such communication exercises, if mastered, will cause us to rise above the fray. So they say.

These suggestions have some merit, but they all deal with the effect rather than the cause. Problems in relationships do not result from poor communication. It's sin. It's always sin, without exception. This is plainly true in marriage. Struggling couples communicate all too well what they are thinking and feeling. Their meaning is clear. The message gets through. There is no mis-communication in marriage. Rather, the mouth speaks precisely what is in the heart. When we do not get along, it is because the mouth spews out the wickedness which has been gathering inside. Don't be distracted by tangential concerns and strategies. There is only one marriage problem—sin.

The Real Relationship Problem

Having said that sin is the only marriage problem, I am tempted to say that there is only one marriage sin—selfishness. The more I live in marriage and counsel marriages, the more I am convinced that almost every struggle, whether big or small, comes down to selfishness on the part of one or both spouses. And I think I have biblical support for this:

> What is the source of quarrels and conflicts among you? Is not the source your pleasures that wage war in your members? You lust and do not have; so you commit murder. You are envious and cannot obtain; so you fight and quarrel. (James 4:1-2)

Although not a passage dealing specifically with marriage, it does speak to relationships. Get this right, and your marriage relationship will be conflict-free. (If you skimmed over the text without really reading it, go back and read it carefully. This is crucial.)

The paragraph begins with the rhetorical question— *What causes quarrels and conflicts?* Did you see it? An inspired writer of the New Testament is asking a question fundamental to human interaction. He is asking, *Why do we fight?* Thankfully, he gives us the answer. We fight because we are selfish.

> *Problems in relationships do not result from poor communication. It's sin. It's always sin, without exception. This is plainly true in marriage.*

Let's move from "we" to "me." *My* selfishness causes *me* to create or maintain quarrels and conflicts. *My* fights with other people originate from a fight within *my* own heart. I want what I want and I am willing to fight my friend, my brother, or my wife to get it.

What this means for you is that whenever you are hurt or upset or angry at your spouse, it is because you are being selfish. You are not getting your way so you take out your frustration on someone else. You desire something ("lust," "envy"), don't have it or cannot get it, so you attack your husband/wife ("commit murder," "fight and quarrel"). This is true *every time* you are hurt or upset or angry at someone else.

You're probably mounting a protest about now. You are preparing your defense thinking, "Not *every* time. There are many times when I am genuinely hurt, when

I have a right to be upset, when he/she really has offended me." And who is your biggest concern in these thoughts? *You*. Your focus is on you. You love you more than anyone else. It is *your* pain, *your* right to be upset, the offense against *you*.

Selfishness in Everyday Marriage

Suppose that my wife says something critical of me. If I get mad and defensive, or I start thinking of all the ways that she is just as bad, or I sulk, or I wallow in self-pity, my concern is for myself not her. If my highest concern were her, I would try to discover the reason for her critical comment. *Is something bothering her that I need to change? Is she reacting to something unrelated to me and taking it out on me? Is she worried about something? Is this just her own selfishness coming out?* Whatever the cause, if I love her I will try to figure it out and do what is best for her. Any other response is love for me.

It goes the other way, too. Suppose I come home an hour late for dinner. The loving, thoughtful thing would have been to call to let her know I would be tardy. But I failed to do that. If she gets upset, treats me with coldness, snaps disrespectfully at me, grumbles, or feels hurt because I did not arrive when she wanted me to, she is being selfish, too. Love and selflessness would include patience and trust, a concern for me and what I was doing. Rather than get upset, she would try to make me glad I did finally come home.

Here is another scenario. I plan a really great date. Every moment has been carefully crafted to maximum *Wow!* factor. I pull it off, hitting the bull's eye perfectly. Her response when all is said and done? "That was nice, thank you." Nice? All of that toil and creativity gets a *Nice*?! "Utterly unacceptable," me thinks. And if my thinking continues down this path of rating her rating of our date, I will soon grow selfish. I will find myself having unkind, uncharitable thoughts of her, becoming sullen or irritated, or worse. It would almost seem that my goal was not to bless her, but to be praised by her. (Which is selfish.)

One more. I say to Krista, "Do you remember when you used to make me that special custard dessert all the time? I really liked that." Krista begins the process of deciding what I meant by that comment. I clearly was not simply reminiscing. She thinks to herself—*He's not happy with me. He wishes I was different. He wants me to be who I was when we got married. I can't. Things change. I changed. What else does he wish was different? He thinks I'm fat now. He thinks all I do is sit around and eat and get fat. That's why he brought up the dessert. He wants me to stop eating dessert so that I can fit into the dresses I wore when we got married. How dare he! I work hard. I never stop, grinding my fingers to the bone, exerting myself to the point of exhaustion. All for him! He doesn't appreciate me. He's trying to change me. He wishes I was someone else. He's an ungrateful, insensitive, overbearing, slave-driving pig who doesn't realize how great he has it. Special custard? Yeah, not in this lifetime, buddy, until you start showing me some respect!*

That may be a little exaggerated, but heading down such a path is self-pitying and egocentric. Love would not allow it. (This is a fictional account, by the way. Krista does not venture very far along such trails without catching herself and turning around.)

Your hurt, frustration, irritation, anger, accusing thoughts, and so on arise from your selfishness. Selfishness is sin. Like all sins, it must be brought to the foot of the cross for forgiveness and repented of. Unchecked selfishness makes one bitter, arrogant, hostile, critical, insensitive, sharp-tongued, and hypocritical. Besides being sin against the Lord, these things make for miserable marriages.

Do not pass by the words "commit murder" too quickly. James picked them on purpose. Our desire to please ourselves at the expense of others is intense. Though we may never actually kill another human being, our attitudes and actions toward others can easily become worthy of the term *homicide*. Husbands and wives do it to each other all the time. As Christians, you both are called to die to yourself and consider others as more important than yourself. This is nowhere more challenging than in marriage.

> *Whenever you are hurt or upset or angry at your spouse, it is because you are being selfish. You are not getting your way so you take out your frustration on someone else.*

Stop & Discuss...

+ Why is it misguided to believe that communication is a significant marriage problem?
+ What does it mean to say, "Sin is the only marriage problem"?
+ Discuss together how hurt feelings, anger, being upset, etc., are all selfish at root.
+ Husband, do you recognize how you act and react selfishly toward her? List a few examples.
+ How about you, wife? Do you recognize it in yourself? Examples?
+ Have you ever considered your selfish treatment of others to be akin to murder? Discuss why that is and how it should affect your view toward your own selfishness.

9

Insights from First Peter

Living With a Disobedient Husband

> In the same way, you wives, be submissive to your own husbands so that even if any of them are disobedient to the word, they may be won without a word by the behavior of their wives, as they observe your chaste and respectful behavior. (1 Peter 3:1-2)

The apostle's instruction in these two verses boils down to this—wives who love and respect contemptible husbands demonstrate Christ-like grace.

Wives are subject to husbands. This is not so much a command as a statement of fact. Men and women are equal in terms of dignity and value, but God has assigned them differing roles in the family. The husband is the head, which means that he has authority over his wife. Again, that is not the way it *should* be, that is the way it is. A husband who fails to act as his wife's authority is like a king who fails to act as ruler. He may be a bad king, a weak king, or a negligent king, but it does not change the fact that he is king.

In 2:18, Peter instructed Christian slaves to submit to their master, even if he was unjust and harsh. That would be a terribly challenging task. Here, he presents a difficult situation which a Christian woman might find herself in—married to an unbelieving man ("disobedient to the word"). Even then she is to submit.

The goal of submission in this case is to win him to Christ. Her means of evangelism is primarily her own devotion to Jesus. "Without a word" does not mean that she should refrain from proclaiming the good news to him. It means that her faithful, obedient life is her greatest asset for getting him to believe the gospel. As she serves Christ, he will notice. If she submits to Christ, she will submit to him, which he will also notice. Basically, the best way to convict her rebellious husband is to model gracious, compliant behavior, to be a fantastic wife without being preachy.

Disobedience is not exclusive to unbelievers. Any Christian can be harsh, unloving, inconsiderate, negligent, and downright mean. So a believing wife married to a believing man has plenty to gain from this passage. Wife, when your husband sins, you will find him generally unwilling to hear about it from you. Even if your accusations are correct, you may find that he turns against you for bringing it up. I recommend that you learn from this text and "win him without a word." After you have gently, respectfully, and lovingly expressed your concerns, let it go. Then become the very best, most satisfying wife you possibly can. Many times, the Spirit of God will use your obedience to Jesus to expose your husband's disobedience. He will eventually come to his senses and repent. And he will be thankful for a wife who loved him even during his failure.

A Wife Who God Treasures

> Your adornment must not be merely external—braiding the hair, and wearing gold jewelry, or putting on dresses; but let it be the hidden person of the heart, with the imperishable quality of a gentle and quiet spirit, which is precious in the sight of God (1 Peter 3:3-4).

Now Peter switches to all wives and explains that godliness is not about getting all done up. (But he is not giving her license to let her appearance go the way of an old, vacant barn either.) Her most appealing qualities will be her character, not her curves, for the simple fact that external beauty is not what distinguishes Christian wives from unbelieving wives. There are gorgeous women in both camps, and there are plain women in both camps.

The Bible does not casually speak of something being *precious* or *valuable* to God, so when a thing is specifically pointed out as such, we ought to sit up and take notice. The gentle, quiet spirit of a wife holds a place of great worth in the divine heart. It sparkles more dazzlingly on a woman than the most expensive jewels. Wife, do not miss this. You can be a unique treasure to God.

One qualification is in order. A "quiet and gentle spirit" is not identical to a "quiet and gentle mouth." I have known (and you have too, no doubt) women who were soft-spoken outside the home, but inside was another story. If you asked their husbands whether these "quiet" wives were gentle and respectful, the honest answer would be a resounding *no!* Conversely, there are women who speak in anything but whispered tones, and yet their delightful service to their husbands is obvious to all, and especially to their man.

> For in this way in former times the holy women also, who hoped in God, used to adorn themselves, being submissive to their own husbands; just as Sarah obeyed Abraham, calling him lord, and you have become her children if you do what is right without being frightened by any fear. (1 Peter 3:5-6)

The Scripture contains several examples of women who were precious to God because of their gracious handling of boneheaded husbands. Their trust was in God, not their spouses. Sarah, for example, submitted to Abraham. The actual word Peter uses is "obeyed" (Gk. *hupakouo*), thereby equating submission and obedience. She even referred to him as "lord" or "master." The one place in the Old Testament which records Sarah calling Abraham *lord* (Gen. 18:12) is not a clear example of her submission to him. But when the entire account of their marriage is considered, her faithful yielding becomes apparent. On not one but two occasions, Abraham presented Sarah to a foreign king as his sister, a move that placed her in the clear and present danger of being violated by the rulers (each time the violation was prevented by the special intervention of God). Nowhere do we find Sarah criticizing Abraham or harboring bitterness toward him or withholding herself from him or speaking ill of him. She was not afraid. She submitted to her lord Abraham because she had full trust in her Lord God.

Consequently, although Sarah was given just one biological child (Isaac), she was given many daughters-in-faith, those who trustingly obey God by submitting to harsh, negligent, or untrustworthy husbands.

A Good Man Knows His Woman

Likewise, husbands, live with your wives in an understanding way, showing honor to the woman as the weaker vessel, since they are heirs with you of the grace of life, so that your prayers may not be hindered. (1 Peter 3:7 ESV)

How should a Christian husband treat his wife? Is he the boss and she his servant? Should he require her to walk two steps behind, speak only when spoken to, and make sure that she does not burn the toast? Sadly, there have been Christian leaders, whole generations even, who have understood headship and submission in that way. A close examination of 1 Peter 3:7 ought to eliminate that cruel misinterpretation forever.

Husbands are described as men who "live with" their wives, a term which the OT uses in connection with the sexual relationship. Although marriage is much more than lovemaking, this verse addresses sex along with the other aspects of wedlock.

Husbands are told to live with their wives (literally) "according to knowledge." A man needs to know his wife. *Knowledge* is an OT term used for, among other things, sexual intimacy. (Again, we will discuss this in detail in a later chapter.) He needs to steadily increase his understanding of what makes her tick. And any wife will tell you that there is a direct link between a husband's seeking to understand her relationally and emotionally and her desire to *know him* physically.

Knowing implies studying. If I want to know how to do a particular skill, I must spend extended periods of time learning about it, examining it, watching others do it, and actually trying it until I achieve the desired knowledge. Desire alone is not enough. Many people would like to know how to play the guitar. But for the ones who never touch a guitar, they might as well say they would like to become a comet. Their chances of doing either is about the same.

As with all relationships, the only way for a man to get to know his wife is by studying her. And, since knowing someone requires conversation, they must talk. He must ask her questions (and listen for the answer). He must learn what she thinks and feels. They must exchange ideas.

Husband, know your wife! Make it a regular goal (regular as in weekly, not yearly) to set aside time exclusively to understand more about her. Get to know her, inside and out. Exert the same effort in learning about her as you do collecting the stats of your favorite player or team. Don't have a greater grasp of your job or hobbies than of what makes your wife happy, sad, jealous, secure, hopeful, depressed, fulfilled, or empty.

> *Any wife will tell you that there is a direct link between a husband's seeking to understand her relationally and emotionally and her desire to know him physically.*

She is Your Co-Heir of Eternal Life

To be called a *vessel* is not a humiliating term, nor is it unique to women. Both men and women are called vessels in the Scripture. We are all instruments in God's hands to do with as He pleases. Also, men as well as women are weak. Remember, Peter referred to women as "weaker," not "weak." There is a difference.

Wives are in the weaker position of submission and, when men actually strive to be men, women are typically weaker physically, emotionally, etc. God's design is for wives to be protected and cared for by their husbands. So Peter's goal is not so much to describe wives as to motivate husbands. He is exhorting men to take up the responsibility and the initiative to understand and cherish their wives. Yes, the wife is commanded to submit to the husband, but this does not mean that he may treat her as his subordinate. A man needs to be tender, patient, and gracious with his wife. He is to treat her with great honor and deference. He should esteem her highly. A wife ought to feel more highly valued than anyone or anything on earth. She is, after all, co-heir of eternal life with him. They share the same destiny. They were bought with the same precious blood of Christ. The Lord Jesus does not regard a wife as inferior, less dignified, or less significant than her husband. Neither should he.

When Peter said that a man's prayers can be hindered, it is difficult to be sure what he means. Is it that God will not listen to the prayers of a man who dishonors and neglects his wife? Or that a man who won't talk to his wife is unlikely to talk to God either? Or both? Either way, a man's failure to honor his wife will result in unanswered prayers. We husbands should consider that very carefully.

Stop & Discuss...

+ Wife, when your husband sins, how do you handle it? Talk about it.
+ Wife, describe for him what you understand a "gentle and quiet spirit" to be.
+ Husband, describe examples of how she manifests this kind of spirit and how she does not.
+ Wife, explain how trusting God will enable you to submit to your husband even if he makes poor choices for you.
+ What does Peter mean by "live with your wife according to knowledge"?
+ Wife, how well does he know you? Do you think he studies you?
+ Husband, do you honor her as a co-heir of eternal life? What does that mean?
+ As you observe marriages in the world, do you see husbands honoring and treasuring their wives? How about in the church? Discuss.

10

A Few Vital Truths

Keep Catching and Getting Caught

To *pursue* is "to chase after, to follow, to go after, to work toward, or to seek." Husband, as a man you are hard-wired to pursue things. It's what men do. We have goals to reach, mountains to climb, adventures to find. We are always in hot pursuit. You convinced a woman to marry you largely by pursuing her. You made her feel special. You convinced her that you will always love and cherish her. You chased after her and trapped her in the net of your love.

Wife, you chose to be trapped. You made yourself attractive to him, hoping to get and keep his attention. You presented yourself inside and out in the way you believed would captivate him. And it worked. He wanted to catch you, and you wanted to get caught.

Don't ever stop! Husband, you should awaken every morning and think, "How can I catch her today?" Wife, you should think, "What do I have to do to make him want to catch me today?" Romance, grace, love, affection, kindness, compassion, conversation, trust, and selflessness must grow and grow over the years. There is no place for waning passion or wilting love in a Christian marriage.

But wane it will if you cease to be intentional in pursuing and wanting to be pursued. Husband, find new ways to woo and wow her. Wife, discover new allurements and enticements which will charm him. Husband, do not turn from this woman to conquer something else (job, hobby, ministry, etc.). Pursue her above all other human relationships and endeavors. Wife, be more appealing and inviting to him than anything else he will encounter throughout the day. Make him believe that he has the perfect wife, and let the future prove that that is what he got. Even during the heavy responsibility of raising children, pursuing each other must remain the higher priority. On your wedding day, you made vows to *each other*, not to your jobs, parents, kids, friends, or other interests. Keep them.

Your Default Setting

Husband, I have asked some questions about how your father did things, and there are more to come. I do this because your default setting is to be a husband like your father is a husband. If he was kind and affectionate to his wife, you are likely to be so with yours. If he was harsh and critical, you will be, too. You need to evaluate your father's husband-habits and evaluate them according to God's design. Where he was good, imitate and improve. Where he was bad, reject and reprogram. Your evaluation of him is not so that you can expose his shortcomings. In fact, I urge you not to do that. The purpose is for the benefit of your marriage and your own husband-habits.

> *There is no place for waning passion or wilting love in a Christian marriage.*

Wife, you are most likely a wife like your mom is a wife. If she speaks in a nagging, disrespectful manner to her husband, you will find yourself doing the same. If she was cold and unloving, your tendency will be similar. Take heart, you *can* change; you *can* overcome. But it rarely happens without conscious effort to be different. You, too, need to evaluate your mother's wifely ways, keeping the good and changing the bad.

Our predisposition to be like our parents is due to the fact that they are the only husband/wife that we have seen up close and personal. Without realizing it, we grow up with the impression, "This is how a husband acts" or "This is the way a wife is." Just knowing that we want to be different changes nothing. We have to know exactly *how* we want to be different and why. Then, we have to be different. Millions of people have said, "I will never be like that," and then continued on just like that.

Choosing to Love Each Other

Love is not something one falls into like a tar pit. Love is a choice. I love Krista because I choose to love her, not because some inexplicable spell came over me rendering me weak in the knees and helplessly drawn to her magnetic enchantments (although, there are times...). I love Krista because I have set my affection on her. If I stop loving her, it will not be because I have fallen out of love, but because I have chosen to set my affection off of her. Love is more about the subject than the object, more about the one loving than the one loved.

On your wedding day, you each chose to set your affection on the other—*forever!* There is no "falling out of love," just falling into sin. Choose to love and to keep loving one another.

Stop & Discuss...

+ Wife, describe for him some of the ways you feel pursued by him. (Husband, take note of what she likes.)
+ Husband, describe what attracts you about her. (Wife, listen and learn.)
+ Discuss marriages you know where they are still in hot pursuit and those who no longer run with passion. What is the difference?
+ If you have kids, discuss how you can keep your marriage a higher priority than parenting. (A general "keep each other first" is not good enough. Be specific.)
+ Husband, if your wife is somewhat like her mother, in what ways are you pleased with that? Displeased?
+ Wife, if your husband is somewhat like his father, in what ways are you pleased with that? Displeased?
+ Discuss how love is a choice and why you will remain "in love" with each other.

11

Top Ten List (Wife)

One night a few years ago, I posed the following question to my bride: "What are the top ten things a typical wife wants?" Without a moment's hesitation she listed them off. I took notes. Then I investigated further with the help of the all-knowing *Google*. Lastly, I asked the opinions of other wives. They all corroborated Krista's original list. Husband, invest the time to memorize and learn this list to see how you can provide each item for your wife. It will be a life-long enterprise, and the specific application of each will change through your different stages of life. Nevertheless, you will both be delighted if you strive to love your wife in each of these areas.

Top Ten Things a Wife Wants

1. Conversation

Your wife wants to talk *with* you, not at you. She wants to discuss her thoughts, activities, desires, fears, experiences, and curiosities. And she wants to hear yours. When you were dating her—trying to win her affections—you had plenty to talk about. If you want to keep her affections, you will find plenty more throughout your marriage.

As mentioned earlier, conversation is the way we get to know someone. Your wife desires to be known by you. And you are commanded to know her, as we saw in 1 Peter 3. It will only happen if you talk. A lot.

Plan regular time for conversation. Plan topics that go beyond the superficial. And be aware that creative, effective question-asking is a skill you will need to hone in order to satisfy this craving of your wife.

I like to divide discussions into three categories.

Level One is the basic life-living conversation where essential facts of our days and existence are discussed. This includes schedules, planning, brief recounting of the day, descriptions of this and that, the general "How's the weather?" kinds of interaction that we need to have just to function in life. These occur several times throughout the week, maybe more than once a day. They can even be held via texting.

Level Two goes deeper into the *whys* and *why it matters*. These discussions cannot be hurried. They require each participant to hear and speak at length. There will be a lot of back-and-forth interactions on just a few topics. You exchange much more than mere words. You gain knowledge of one another and express loving concern. They usually take place over coffee or a meal. You have to sit near one another where you can see the other's face, with all distractions (like electronic devices) far away. These may not occur every day, but they must happen at least once a week.

Level Three is the most exhausting and the most rewarding level. These conversations are infrequent, but deeply beneficial and satisfying. They usually involve tears. They require extended periods of uninterrupted time to allow for each participant to think long and deep about something, then to express those thoughts. They often include sustained silence, heart explorations, and unresolved questions. They may be planned, to tackle a significant issue in the marriage or family, or they may be somewhat spontaneous, in response to a major and unanticipated event. Either way, they must not be rushed or cut off prematurely. (I have found that getaways are ideal settings for Level Three conversations.)

Husband, make sure that all three levels receive the proper attention needed to bless and know your wife.

You will also need to master the art of listening. I mean *really* listening, as opposed to the occasional nod and random "Uh huh," as your mind wanders to a land far, far away. She knows when your mind drifts. You are not fooling her. It is rude. It conveys that she is not worth your time, that something else is more valuable to you. But listening well, remembering what she says, interacting with what she says, and acting on what she says, conveys that you do cherish and love her. Remember, a cherished wife wants to please her husband, so expend great effort to maintain a vibrant and frequent talking relationship.

You will probably come up against many challenges as you seek regular conversations with your wife. You may think you're too busy (translation: other things have become more important than your wife). Your wife may become less interesting (translation: you have let the relationship dissolve). Perhaps other people or pursuits excite you more. Or, the one that plagues us all, you may become too self-centered to talk to her.

These, and more, emerge as life endures, but there are ways to avoid them or at least to minimize their impact. Work toward the following preventions and solutions:

+ *Keep less important activities from your schedule.* If you engage in other things at the expense of regular conversations together, the cost is too high. Adjust your calendars accordingly.

+ *Look for admirable qualities and abilities in her.* She has plenty of them. Notice them and tell her you noticed. (And tell others in her hearing!)

+ *Plan regular times of conversation.* Meals, dates, car rides, walks, etc., should be intentionally incorporated into your weekly routine and used for talking together. If you truly have nothing to say to your wife, you are in trouble.

+ *Do not pursue "dangerous" relationships.* Any association with friends, family, or others which detracts or distracts from your wife is dangerous. Let them go and pursue her.

+ *Regularly pray for a selfless heart toward your wife.* When you love yourself more than her, only the Spirit of God can help. Seek Him.

Stop & Discuss...

+ Wife, explain why you enjoy talking with him.
+ Wife, does he ever ignore you or "tune you out" while you are talking? If so, describe an example and tell him how you feel when he does that.
+ Discuss together the potential obstacles and challenges listed above, along with the potential solutions.

2. Physical Affection

Your wife wants you to hold her hand, to hug her, to rest your hand on her thigh while driving, to stroke her hair and skin, to come up behind her at the sink and embrace, to rub her back, shoulders, and feet. She wants to be touched. With the rare exception of those who are bitter or those who have been traumatized by abuse, a wife desires to be in regular contact with her husband's body.

Every woman is different, so you will have to learn where and how your wife enjoys being touched. But continual caressing expresses your desire to be near her. Touching is intimate, usually reserved for those we trust and want to be close to. Show her often how much you want to be close to her.

Please note that this kind of touching is without obvious sexual intent. Sometimes, she wants to be touched in a way that says, "I want to be next to you and touching you simply because I love you," rather than "Can we have sex now?" If you only touch her in bed or when you are wanting to go to bed, she will feel used, not loved. On the other hand, frequent non-sexual touching often leads to frequent sexual touching. It is one of the beautiful paradoxes of marriage.

> *Invest the time to memorize and learn this list to see how you can provide each item for your wife...it will be a life-long enterprise...begin on your wedding day and strive to love your wife in each of these areas.*

Stop & Discuss...

+ Discuss how physically affectionate your parents were at home and in public. How would you like to be like them?
+ Wife, describe the kinds of physical affection that you like and why.
+ Husband, what would cause you not to want to touch your wife? Why?

3. Verbal Encouragement

A woman wants to be affirmed in her work as a mother and as a wife and as a pianist (or whatever else she does). She wants to know that you approve of her efforts. Second only to the Lord, she wants to please you. She desperately wants to be *told* that you are pleased. This one takes very little time and effort on your part, but its impact is tremendous.

Consider what the Scripture says about the power of words:

> *Pleasant words are a honeycomb,*
> *Sweet to the soul and healing to the bones.*
> *~ Proverbs 16:24*

A soothing tongue is a tree of life,
But perversion in it crushes the spirit.
~ Proverbs 15:4

Death and life are in the power of the tongue.
~ Proverbs 18:21

The tongue is a fire, the very world of iniquity...and is set
on fire by hell...no one can tame the tongue; it is a restless evil
and full of deadly poison. With it we bless our Lord and
Father, and with it we curse men, who have been made in the
likeness of God...these things ought not to be this way.
~ James 3:6-10

Do you realize what all of this means for you? You have the ability to heal your wife's bones, to sweeten her soul, and to lead her to the tree of life just in what you say and how you say it. You can invigorate and energize her through your words. Or you can crush her, dampen her spirits, wound her soul, and virtually kill her with your words. You have been given a powerful tool. Use it to build rather than to destroy.

In a typical marriage, the proportion of critical, demeaning, grumbling, and harsh words to affirming, dignifying, grateful, and tender words is usually about 100 to 1. Don't be typical. Show how precious she is by using carefully constructive and supportive language.

A special word about sarcasm. Most women hate it. Even those who use it usually do not really enjoy it. They may fire right back at you, or laugh when you ridicule them, or act like it's just a game. But often, those who enter into verbal sparring on the outside are weeping and wounded on the inside. Husband, eliminate mocking, derision, ridicule, and harsh joking from your relationship. Speak only kind, gentle, uplifting words to your bride.

Stop & Discuss...

+ Talk about a time when you have been destroyed by the words of another, and when you have been built up by someone's words.
+ Describe marriages you have seen where either spouse regularly cuts down the other. Why do they do that? What are the results?
+ Describe marriages where the spouses regularly build up one another.
+ Wife, describe to your husband how his words impact you.

4. Help Around the House/With Kids

Whether your wife works mostly inside or outside the home, she will appreciate your assistance in the home. If she spends 45 minutes putting the kids to bed while you build endurance in your "phone thumb," do not expect her to come sit next to you with a gleam in her eye. Don't deceive yourself into thinking that you "deserve" or "need" to relax, as if your day was more stressful than hers. You are a team, partners, one flesh. Yes a husband and wife have different responsibilities and duties, and a godly wife will find joyful satisfaction in homemaking, still, one of the significant ways a husband cherishes his wife is by giving her a break (or even sharing the load).

Vacuuming, washing the dishes, de-cluttering, etc., can be wonderful expressions of love. Cooking is good, too. Basically, anything that will keep you from being lazy while she labors will be well received.

Stop & Discuss...

+ Discuss together how your fathers helped your mothers in the home and with the kids.
+ Wife, how would you like your husband to be like your father? Unlike?

5. Security

You probably expect this topic to be about economic or temporal provision. And it is. But there are three others areas of security that are even more important to a wife. We will discuss all four briefly.

Security (or lack thereof) will have a tremendous impact on your relationship. If your wife feels secure, she will be free and uninhibited to love you. If insecure, she will be tense, restrained, and anxious. I urge you to make her feel secure in each of these ways.

Financial Security. Your wife wants to know that you will take care of her and your family today and tomorrow. And the day after that. And the one after that. She knows that God is ultimately her provider, but she also knows that He has given you the responsibility to take care of her.

Here are some practical ways to promote security in your wife:

+ *Do not spend money foolishly.* Prove that you will spend with wisdom and forethought rather than impulsively and thoughtlessly. Get-rich schemes, lotto tickets, and debt accumulation do not foster financial trust.

+ *Stay within your budget.* (You *must* have a budget.) Budgets are like diets, they only help if you actually stay on them.

+ *Make prudent financial and career decisions.* No one can predict the future, and the Lord's direction must always be our greatest concern. Yet Jesus wants us to use our brains. Don't go in directions that will cause unnecessary stress and strain on your wife's heart. Your destiny is hers as well. Assure her that you care about both.

✦ *Do not give your wife reason to worry about your financial situation, present or future.* Life brings plenty of opportunities to test your wife's trust in the Lord without you making it the norm. Occasionally, God calls us to take great steps of faith. When He does, you must go for it while helping your wife to rest in His provision. But don't put Him to the test or put her in unnecessary financial risk.

Stop & Discuss...

✦ Wife, did your mother trust her husband to make wise financial decisions? Explain.
✦ Do you have any concerns about how your husband handles finances? Talk about it.
✦ Husband, are you financially responsible? Is your wife secure? Defend your answer.

Relational Security. More than simply entrusting you with her money, your wife has entrusted you with her life. By committing to you, she chose a course for everything that matters to her. If you betray her or disappoint her, it will be of monumental consequence. Be trustworthy. Be dependable. Always.

+ *Give your wife no reason to suspect your unfaithfulness.* This will overlap with another item on the list below, but it bears repeating. Do whatever it takes for her to live beyond any reasonable doubt of your fidelity.

+ *Divorce is not a possibility. Never! Not gonna happen! No way! I will not abandon you, period!* She needs to believe that from the very bottom of her heart.

+ *Make sure that she feels like the top of your priority list.* The emphasis is on her *feeling* it. You may convince yourself that she is number one, but convincing her is the goal. She should believe that given the choice between her and anyone or anything else, you will choose her every time.

+ *Know what she perceives to be possible threats to your marriage.* This requires awareness on your part because she may not articulate it to you freely. Still, you need to be alert to her concerns. Your goal is to alleviate any fears she may have about your relationships with other women, friends, family, career, ministry, or other interests.

Stop & Discuss...

+ Wife, do you have any doubts or
  concerns about his faithfulness?
  Explain it to him.
+ Do you currently feel threatened
  by anything or anyone?

Spiritual Security. Your wife also wants to feel safe in how you lead her and your family to please God. You are her Christ-representative and spiritual head. She wants a worthy, strong leader.

+ *Give her no reason to doubt your love for, and devotion to, Christ.* Her greatest source of comfort in you is your commitment to the Lord Jesus. If you remain faithfully devoted to Him, you will remain faithfully devoted to her. If your allegiance to Him wanes, there is no telling what you might do to her. Make Christ your highest priority and your wife will be at ease.

+ *Lead her (and your children) in serving, studying, praying, etc.* You do not have to get a theology degree or learn Greek and Hebrew in order to lead your wife in spiritual things. But you do have to lead her. It is your privilege as head of the home to take charge of your household's commitment to Christ and the exercise of the spiritual disciplines. Make a plan and implement it. I encourage you to seek the advice of other husbands and fathers to determine what approaches will be most beneficial.

+ *Let her observe you praying, studying, and serving.* Part of leadership is setting an example for others to follow. Your wife needs to see you loving Christ and His people.

+ *Be the same person at home and at church.* Hypocrisy does not breed security. If you put on a good show at church or at small group meetings, but turn into a totally different character when you leave the parking lot, your wife will have reason for genuine concern (not to mention the Lord's displeasure). Be a real Christian, committed to growing in grace and knowledge. Deceit will force her to distrust you.

If your wife feels secure, she will be free and uninhibited to love you. If insecure, she will be tense, restrained, and anxious.

Stop & Discuss...

+ Do you currently read the Bible together? Pray together? Serve together? How can you improve in each of these areas?
+ Wife, are you following your husband in these things? Describe to him how you would like him to lead in spiritual areas.
+ Husband, what are your greatest challenges in spiritual leadership? How can you overcome them?
+ Describe for each other how your fathers led well or poorly. How did your mothers respond to their leadership?

Family Security. One of the reasons she married you was because she thought you would be a great father to your children. Make her glad she said yes (assuming you have kids).

+ *Assure her of your love for your children.* She will not be secure in your love or your ability to lead your family if you despise or dislike your kids.

+ *Make sure she understands that you discipline the children out of love, not anger.* Firm discipline, spanking, and other training virtues are required of Christian parents. Your wife will follow your lead as long as she is convinced that you have their best in mind. But remember, she is their mother, feeling a deep sense of responsibility to nurture and protect them. Don't cause her to feel that she has to protect them from you.

+ *Make wise decisions regarding your children.* In all areas of life—discipline, schooling, church participation, choosing babysitters, bedtime, the number of toys they are allowed to own, whether to get immunizations, everything— you are responsible for your family. In each case, lead intelligently, gaining the necessary knowledge and counsel to make good decisions.

+ *Do not exasperate your children.* Fathers can do this in two ways: either by being too stern and overbearing or by being too lenient and passive. Both prove seriously detrimental to the child. Grow in wisdom regarding child-rearing. Be sensitive to their spirits and demeanor. Do not crush them. Do not be manipulated by them. As with your wife, sarcasm and cut-downs will only damage them. Build them into joyful servants of Christ.

✦ *Be a father, not merely a provider.* Working eighty hours a week so that you can give your kids everything you never had is sin. What your kids need is a dad who will spend time with them teaching, nurturing, loving, encouraging, and leading. Many things have to be sacrificed when a man becomes the head of a home. Give them up cheerfully and raise your kids. Your wife will be comforted to see it.

Stop & Discuss...

✦ How did your fathers teach and discipline his kids? Talk about it.
✦ Were your fathers heavily involved at home, largely absent from the home, or somewhere in between?
✦ Wife, in what ways would you like your husband to be like your father as a parent? In what ways would you like him to be different? Discuss together.

6. Time Together

Husband, why was she willing to marry you? What did she want? Among other things, she wanted to be with you all the time. She still wants that. Just being near you, wherever you are, will make her smile.

When you were dating, you enjoyed hanging out with her for hours. Don't let that ever change. Make time to be with your wife, and be intentional about enjoying it.

If you look at the marriages around you (or come sit in my office for a few marriage counseling sessions), you will see many couples who have lost that never-want-to-be-apart-from-each-other joy. You do not have to lose it, but you will unless you are determined and purposeful. You must plan regular time together (at least weekly). Not merely time in the same house or the same room, but time for uninterrupted, unhurried, relationship-building interaction.

Opportunities are all around—early morning coffee before work, walks in the park or neighborhood, sitting together before bed, date nights, doing a hobby together, sitting on the back porch or deck, sending the kids to their room so that you can be alone together— but they will not just happen, they must be *taken*. Form these habits now and maintain them throughout your marriage.

Stop & Discuss...

+ Wife, explain why you like to be with him.
+ Discuss how much time your parents spent together, just the two of them.
+ Wife, would you welcome more time together with your man? Explain.
+ Husband, what are you willing to give up to give your wife more of your time?

7. Faithfulness

Your wife wants to be sure that you would never trade her in on a newer or more attractive model. She craves confirmation that you would not abandon her for anything or anyone. Wandering eyes, flirtation with other gals, disinterest in her, lack of sexual desire for her, and other such things will cause your wife to doubt. Your job is to leave her no room for doubt. Devote yourself only to her, and make it obvious that she, and she alone, has your heart, soul, eyes, and body.

Here are a few more specific suggestions:

+ *Do not have threatening relationships with other women.* By God's grace, I have remained faithful to my wife in mind, heart, and body since the day we got married (August 15, 1992). I have no desire to be with any other woman. I love my wife. I give thanks for her every day. I cannot imagine being more happily married. I have the world's greatest wife and would be an utter fool to think that another woman, no matter how attractive or appealing at first glance, would be an improvement. Still, I am a sinful human being who lives with the potential to do utterly foolish things. Thus, one axiom I strive to live by is, *Greater men than me have fallen.* I take great pains not to put myself in a situation where I could be tempted to fall.

+ *I do not maintain close relationships with other women unless Krista is also part of those relationships.* I do not go out to eat or drive in a car with another woman unless others are also present. When I do counseling with a woman, my staff knows it and pays attention (they walk the halls), and my blinds are always open. Krista always has my current calendar so that she knows who I am with and where. I share as much as I can with her without breaking confidence. I welcome her questions about my interactions with other women. All of this and more is part of my desire to protect my heart and my marriage. I exhort you to maintain equally strict measures of protection. You need it, and she wants it.

+ *Do not let your eyes follow the pretty gals walking by.* Yes, I said earlier that seeing a beautiful woman is not sin. But don't be stupid or insensitive. All other women should go largely unnoticed.

+ *Do not flirt with other women.* Being married does not require you to be rude and unfriendly with the rest of the female population. It does require you to save the charming, wooing, sweet-talking magnetism solely for your bride. Give your girl assurance that your only interest in other girls is righteous, Christian, sisterly love.

+ *Do not talk about other women, real or imagined, as if allured by them.* You are only allowed to be captivated by one woman. Make sure she knows that you are only captivated by her. If she thinks that she is in competition with another person (or a fantasy in your head), she will be insecure. (And rightfully so, since your love for her is not secure). Your devotion is to her and her alone. Talk only of her.

Stop & Discuss...

+ Wife, does he flirt, stare at pretty women, or anything else that bothers you? Do you have any doubts about his faithfulness? Tell him about it.
+ Does he have any other relationships that make you feel uneasy?
+ Husband, are you willing to do whatever will make her feel at ease?
+ Are you taking the necessary measures to prevent dangerous situations? Describe what that looks like.
+ Discuss how your fathers demonstrated and maintained faithfulness to their wife.

8. Time to Herself

This is true in proportion to the number (and age) of kids in the home. God has designed wives to be home-oriented. But they will be better homemakers if they get out of the house now and then. Your wife should have regular time (directed and initiated by you) doing "her thing." If you have young kids, this means not doing her thing with junior tagging along. An occasional overnight away by herself or with friends is also a good idea. (You plan it for her!)

Recommendations:

- Buy her gift cards to Starbucks, then help her make time to use them.

- Make arrangements for the kids. If you leave childcare up to her, it may never happen.

- Send her on an overnight personal retreat. Time alone to read, pray, study, plan, rest, recharge, etc., is good for all of us. Women (especially those who are servant-hearted) typically will not take the initiative to withdraw and rejuvenate. You should initiate for her. Make reservations at a nice getaway spot. Give her a prepaid credit card to spend on herself. Help her plan how to spend her time. Arrange a trip to the spa. Do whatever will make it a special and profitable time for her.

- Convince her to enjoy this personal time. Her instinct will be to feel guilty for being away from you (all the more so if you have children at home). You need to help her feel free to enjoy herself. Encourage her. Help her see the benefit. Persuade her of your support.

Stop & Discuss...

+ Did your mothers ever have time to themselves? If not, why not? If so, what did they do? How did it benefit them?
+ Wife, do you feel like you need time to yourself? Explain.
+ Husband, can you explain to her why she may need it and how it may benefit her?

9. A Husband Who Takes Care of Himself

Husband, what shape are you in? No, you don't have to maintain a certain BMI or six-pack abs, but your wife wants to know that you are going to be around to take care of her for decades. She understands that our days are in the Lord's hands, but she will be comforted if you are doing everything you can humanly speaking to live a long and healthy life. So, enjoy God's good gifts, but don't become a glutton.

This maintenance goes beyond fitness. Good hygiene is a plus, since no one likes bad breath and body odor. She also wants you to pursue intellectual growth. Read some books. Learn some new things. Expand your abilities. Have some drive, passion, and vision. And don't allow stress to endanger your health. Lead the way in trusting the Lord and handling trials with faith and hope. Grow and maintain as much spiritual, physical, and mental strength as you can. She will find that comforting and attractive.

Stop & Discuss...

+ Discuss how your fathers took care of themselves (or didn't).
+ What is the difference between being a good steward of our mind/body and being obsessed? Do you know people who are one or the other?
+ Wife, do you have any fears regarding your husband's self-care? Describe them to him.

10. Chocolate

I recognize that there are a handful of women out there who do not like chocolate, and your wife may be one of them. But what chocolate represents your wife *does* like. I'm talking about romance. She wants to be wooed, pursued, courted, dated, chased after, wined and dined, and all the other cliches expressing that special interest you have shown her throughout your dating/courtship period. The things that won her heart in the first place must continue and increase throughout your marriage. Lavish good gifts and alluring adoration upon her with vim and vigor. Romance your wife!

Here are some helpful tips:

1. Dating is for married people. The world has it all backward. Leading up to marriage, one's time ought to be spent in careful, sober reflection about the seriousness of the marriage commitment and the person to whom he or she is about to commit. Passion and romance should be parked (or at least stay in first gear) until after the "I do's," when it accelerates as the natural expression of growing love. But most couples fan the flame before the wedding, then do the careful reflecting later (sometimes in the form of "What have I done?"). Too often the flame reduces to flicker.

Your marriage will be different if you learn and practice the art of married dating. Yes, it is an art form. That's good news. Arts and skills are things which can be honed. Your dating ability can be developed and improved. You can learn to be a good dater, a skill I earnestly commend to you. Done right, it will become a regular passion-generator for your marriage.

But like all skills, good dating takes work. Notice that I said *good* dating. Anyone can throw something together. But to do this well requires commitment and practice. If you are going to become a good dater, you must be willing to:

- Study your wife carefully.

- Do some serious research.

- Make reservations, purchase gifts, etc.

- Bring your creativity out of hibernation and put it to use.

- Learn how to do some new things.

- Engage in lots of fun projects.

Good dating also takes time. It cannot be accomplished in the five minutes before the date starts. ("What would you like to do tonight, Honey?" is the cardinal sin of dating. Do not ever say it or anything like it again!) Good dates start days, sometimes months, before the actual event. It requires advance planning. Planning takes time.

Good dating also requires time for the dates. Despite our best intentions, many marriages let all sorts of less important things take priority over the relationship. It is easy for a husband to say that his wife is at the top of his list while choosing week after week to fill his calendar with something or someone else. Consistent dating can reverse this trend.

Good dating is fun. Krista and I have a regular weekly date, and we love it. We look forward to it. As the husband, it is my privilege to do most of the planning for it. Rather than being a chore every week, it is a wonderful time. Sure, a babysitter is expensive and life is busy, but by spending our time and money in this way we prove the value we place on our marriage. Don't get me wrong, our devotion to dating is not merely a "principled decision," we crave it. You will, too, if you do it well.

2. Spend money on your wife. I have seen it many times. The husband is budget-conscious (obsessed?) when it comes to buying gifts for his wife, but he finds the funds to play golf or buy the newest gadget or go hunting or.... The message is received loudly and clearly by his wife—he has money to do what he wants to do and she is not it.

With all the proper qualifications regarding stewardship and financial wisdom admitted, *spend money on your wife!* Take her on dates. Buy jewelry. Go clothes shopping with her. See a movie in the theater once in a while (one that she likes). Prepay for the next book in the series that she has been reading. Send her surprise packages from *Amazon*. Shell out a few bucks for the person you say you love more than anyone or anything else.

3. Romance her on days besides the expected ones. Without exception, your wedding anniversary should be marked out for a special celebration of your marriage. And Valentine's Day has become a staple. Romance your wife on these days. But in addition to these, surprise her with unannounced gifts and romantic events. Special dates, weekend getaways, extended trips, expensive dinners, and whatever else you can come up with should not be reserved exclusively for the calendar-driven festivities.

4. Be creative. Lazy routine can be a romance killer. (I said "lazy" because well-planned patterns—like weekly date nights—can be fun for her to anticipate). Rousing romance will flow from imaginative consideration of how you can bless your wife. Put some time and thought into it. Invent ways, experiment a little, be resourceful and adventurous. Endeavor to find new ways to cherish the love of your life.

5. Keep your eyes and ears open for what she likes. Women lie to us. Not intentionally or maliciously, but still, you cannot always trust what you hear. For example, many years ago Krista suggested that I stop buying flowers for her. "They just die," she said. "I don't need them. I would rather you spend money on something more substantial, more enduring," she persuaded. *Lies! All of it.* You see, I believed her and proceeded to not buy her flowers for a year or so. Then one day a woman in the church brought her a bouquet as an expression of gratitude. Krista went on and on and on. And on. She loved the flowers. I caught her red-handed when she was on the phone telling her friend how beautiful they were, how pleasant they smelled, how they lit up the room with life and joy.

The real point here is that you need to be alert to what romances her. Listen up when she tells someone that she would like to see a movie or eat at a restaurant or go to a musical performance. Start a "date and gift" list and keep adding to it. Take notes when watching chick flicks. Ask other romantic husbands for ideas. Put a weekly planning hour on your calendar where you strategize and design your romantic schemes for the next 7-10 days.

Stop & Discuss...

+ Wife, name one thing he has done in your marriage that was really romantic.
+ What other things do you find romantic and special?
+ I said, "What would you like to do tonight, Honey?" is the cardinal sin of dating. Husband, do you understand why? Discuss this together.
+ Husband, why does romance take time? Are you putting the time in? Ask your wife how she would grade your efforts.
+ Discuss how your fathers were or were not regularly romantic.
+ Wife, tell him what it would mean to you for him to learn the arts of dating and romance. (Or if he already knows them, how grateful you are.)

12

Top Ten List (Husband)

Wife, your husband has desires and expectations of you just as you have of him. If you become fluent and skilled at the following ten things, he will be a happy man who wants to cherish you. Use this as a guide for knowing how to please and serve your man.

Top Ten Things a Husband Wants

1. Respect

This has to do with the honor and submission appropriate for a Christian woman toward her husband. Your husband has been given authority over you and responsibility for you. He is your head, your provider, your protector. He is called to love you sacrificially and selflessly. As a man entrusted with such a high position, he very much desires to be honored by you, the one for whom he will discharge these duties. Your job is to recognize his authority and treat him appropriately. A husband cannot feel like a godly husband if his wife is disrespectful.

As mentioned earlier, the most effective instrument you have for showing respect is your mouth. It is also your most effective instrument for showing disrespect. Be careful with your words.

Here are some examples of how a wife disrespects her husband:

+ *Criticism.* Expressing that he falls short of *your* standards (as if that is what he should be striving for).

+ *Commanding him to do things.* ("Go start the car!" "Go get the kids!" "Turn off the TV!" "Let's go!" "Feed the dog!")

+ *Telling him what he needs to do.* ("You need to cut the grass." "You should stop....")

+ *Telling him what to say on the phone* (dictating and correcting in the background).

+ *Side-seat driving.*

+ *Treating him like he is your child* (or more condescendingly than you treat your kids).

Some wives order their husband around, tell him what to do, take control of situations—essentially assuming headship of the home—and then complain because their husband will not be the head. She emasculated him, and then complains that he is not masculine. This is sin! Wife, never speak to your husband in a way that you would not speak to Christ.

Here are some examples of respect:

+ *Ask, don't command.* ("Would you mind warming up the car, Hunk-o-mine?" "Do you think we should leave for church soon?" "I would really like to stop by the store on our way. Could we please do that?")

+ *Be consciously aware of the fact that you are under his authority and speak to him accordingly.*

+ *Look for ways to encourage his "successes" and look past his failures.* Commend his good decisions and build him up after bad ones.

+ *Make sure that your tone is always respectful and humble, not condescending or critical.* Again, your tone should be no different than if you were speaking to Jesus.

+ *Don't talk when he is on the phone* (unless you are distracting him with suggestions of how handsome you think he is).

+ *Express appreciation for his leadership, protection, provision, and love.* (There will be many things to appreciate. If you cannot think of any, you are not looking hard enough.)

✦ *Pray for him and for his responsibilities as your head.* (Pray in his hearing or send emails sharing your prayers for him.)

Stop & Discuss...

✦ Husband, can you think of anything she has said or done recently that felt disrespectful to you? Talk about it.
✦ Describe how your mothers showed respect/disrespect to their husband.
✦ Wife, do you understand why it is inappropriate for you to give orders to your husband? Explain it to him.
✦ Discuss marriages you observe where respect from the wife to the husband is obvious, and where it is obviously missing. How do you think the husbands feel in each case?
✦ Wife, what is your greatest challenge in respecting your husband? Does he agree? Talk about it.

2. Admiration

A husband wants to know that his wife approves of him, that she is impressed by him. He longs to believe that she has "That's *my* husband!" moments. He wants her to swell with pride regarding his achievements, work, abilities, characteristics, etc. He wants to feel like his wife would not trade him for any other man, even if it were allowed.

Admiration tips:

✦ *Tell him how good he is at something or how he blesses others, and be specific.* I spend many hours of every week in sermon preparation formulating a message that I hope will honor Christ and have a profoundly positive impact on His people. It is my craft and calling. It is an exceedingly significant part of who I am. Every Sunday on the way home from church, I wait anxiously for Krista's review of my work. I want to know what my bride thinks of my "creation." I long to receive her praise (or, sometimes, her suggestions for improvement). She also comments on my counseling, leadership, insights, patience, diligence, etc. She expresses how blessed she is that I am her husband and the father of our children. She looks for ways to encourage me and praise my accomplishments. Your husband longs to hear such things from you.

✦ *Tell others of his admirable qualities or efforts in front of him.* A man tries not to brag, but he feels like a king when his wife brags on him.

He may play it down as a matter of "humility," but inside he will be flying high.

+ *Tell your children of the many wonderful things about their father.*

+ *Pray and give thanks for him while he is listening.* Hearing you voice gratitude to God for him will cause your husband to feel greatly appreciated and admired.

+ *Ask for his help.* Husbands feel admired when they are sought out for assistance. It tells us not only that we are needed, but that our wives know that they need us.

All of this will require you to look for the good in him and to look past the bad.

A final note on the difference between respect and admiration. According to the dictionary, they are basically synonyms. However, I am using them to describe two related but different ideas. To put it simply and succinctly, when you think of respecting your husband, think "Aye aye, captain!" and of admiration, think "You're my hero!"

Stop & Discuss...

+ Wife, explain the difference between respect and admiration as we are using the terms.
+ Do your mothers admire their husband? Explain and discuss.
+ Admiration comes easy at the beginning of most relationships. Why? And why does it become harder as time goes by?
+ What does admiration from a wife to a husband look like? Have you seen it?
+ Husband, do you feel admired by your wife? Tell her about it.

3. A Wife Who Doesn't Nag or Complain

To nag is to constantly annoy and irritate by repeatedly bringing up the same thing or persistently pointing out the same faults.

Husbands hate nagging. *Really* hate it. It is one of the main opponents of meaningful conversation because a man who is nagged feels disrespected and belittled. Who wants to pursue loving affection or deep discussion with a woman who is always criticizing or yapping or carping or hounding or grumbling?

Here is what the wise King Solomon (a man of some experience with wives) had to say about it:

It is better to live in a corner of the housetop
than in a house shared with a quarrelsome wife.
~ Proverbs 21:9

Tips to avoid and overcome nagging:

+ *Once you have expressed your desire, let it go.* After your husband knows about it, when and how he deals with it is subject to his discretion. Keeping on him will only create tension and frustration.

+ *Ask yourself why you feel the need to nag.* Maybe you have sins of control-freak-ness, bitterness, impatience, or unkindness that need to be repented of.

+ *Ask the Holy Spirit to reveal your nagging and to help you stop.*

+ *Recognize the damage you are doing to your marriage through your nagging.*

+ *Study and meditate on 1 Peter 3:1-6.* We already considered this passage in chapter 9. Review it regularly and prayerfully.

Stop & Discuss...

+ Husband, explain what she or someone else does that feels like nagging to you.
+ What would you really like her to understand about nagging?
+ Did your mothers nag their husband? Describe.
+ Wife, what are you likely to grumble and complain about? How can you prevent it?

---

4. Trust

A man wants to be trusted by his wife. He wants to be assured that no one knows her better than he, that she is more vulnerable with him than with any other person. To put it another way, spouses are intended to be "naked and unashamed" with one another. A wife who is unwilling to expose the deepest parts of her soul to him, or to express her most intimate thoughts and feelings to him, does not trust him. He wants to be her help, guidance, and comfort because he is Christ's earthly representative. If she doesn't trust him, he can't become these things.

Trust is the basic requirement for intimate relationship. Many wives who long to be closer to their husband prevent it by refusing to trust him, which eliminates the possibility for closeness. Trust is a choice. Many husbands become jealous, callous, or defeated by an untrusting wife.

Trust is conveyed when you rely on him and when you assume the best of his motives and abilities. Do not doubt him. Do not question him (which is different from asking questions). Communicate how much you believe in him.

Stop & Discuss...

+ Husband, does she trust you? Explain to her how she does or does not express trust in you.
+ Did your mothers trust their husband? Discuss.
+ Husband, tell her how important it is to you that she trust you.
+ Wife, what is your greatest struggle in trusting him?

5. Physical Affection (Not Just Overtly Sexual)

Men enjoy the touch of a woman. Wife, make sure that your man enjoys yours regularly.

Preferences vary, so you will have to do some exploration. For example, I like Krista's hand on my thigh when I'm driving. I like when she takes my hand when we are walking. I love it when she reaches over in the car and strokes the back of my head. I *do not* like her to caress my arm or fingers. Examine him. Learn what pleases him. Then, do it. Touch him! (If you do not like to touch your husband, you need to determine why. It may be an indicator of significant issues that need attention.)

Many men also feel admired when their wives are affectionate with them in public. It says, "I am with this guy, and proud of it. He's *my* man."

Stop & Discuss...

+ Husband, tell her what you like about being touched.
+ Do you like public affection? Why?
+ Did your mothers initiate affection with your fathers? Discuss.
+ Wife, what causes you not to want to touch him?

6. Companionship in Work, Hobbies, Pursuits, Etc.

A husband wants his wife to take interest in his interests. He likes to have her near and, depending on the activity, participating with him. When you were dating, the two of you did almost everything together. You are willing to try new things, share new experiences, go to new places. He enjoyed your company. He will still enjoy it now if you prove to be a fun and encouraging mate.

How to be a companion:

+ *Support him in his hobbies, work, interests.* Go to the driving range with him. Drive the cart. Walk if you don't play golf. Inquire about his latest pastime. Do things that you don't particularly like to do just to be with him.

+ *Learn something new together.* You may not enjoy everything your husband does, but be willing to expand your comfort zone. Be his partner in an activity that he especially wants to do.

+ *Be excited when he returns from doing something, and ask about it (golf, running, fishing, hiking, whatever).* Krista does not play golf. In fact, we tried it once and decided our marital bliss might be in jeopardy if we continued. Yet, she still shows great interest in my golf playing. When I get home, she requests to hear about my game. She wants details. She inquires about every hole, every drive, every putt. I know that she does not care that much about the game itself, but her asking shows that she cares that much about *me*. I like to know that.

+ *Surprise him by purchasing something for his hobbies.* Is he a hiker? Go with him to REI and take notes on something you can purchase for him later as a gift. Musician? Find a live video of his favorite artist. Learn about his various interests enough to invest in them and encourage him.

+ *Don't badger him or complain about it.* It is selfish for a wife to guilt her husband out of doing things he likes. If you love him, you will want him to please himself sometimes.

Stop & Discuss...

+ Husband, what would you like for her to participate in with you?
+ Teach her how she can show interest in your activities and hobbies.
+ Discuss how your mothers were successful or unsuccessful in this area.
+ Wife, are you willing to try new things if it will make him happy?
+ What is your biggest struggle in this area?

7. Conversation About Non-Trivial Things (Minimal Chatter)

It is not that husbands don't like to talk or that we have "less words" than women. (Sorry to betray the secret, guys, but that is a myth created to let men off the hook.) Rather, we typically do not enjoy listening to a long series of random, disconnected, apparently irrelevant sentence fragments. We *do* enjoy conversations where our opinions are respected and which stay in the same zip code as they began. For some men, the perceived pointlessness of his wife's rambling proves exhausting but tolerable. For others, it seems outright disrespectful (as though she just wants to talk, rather than wanting to talk *to him* about something specific.)

Wife, you should also understand that your husband's desire to converse with you is directly tied to 1) whether he feels respected and admired by you, 2) how much you nag him, and 3) how passionate you are about sex with him (which we will discuss a little further down). A man is happy to talk with a person who does not tear him down, criticize him, or belittle him. He will joyfully engage in deep discussions with you if you respect his opinions, admire his abilities, and show your love for him in lovemaking. He will not want to talk with a wife who nags, condemns, makes him feel unimportant, or refuses to be sexual. It's all tied together. One of the major reasons a man will talk at length to his friend or brother but not with his wife is that he feels respected and appreciated by them. They don't nag, complain, or denigrate. Or ramble. (Okay, some do. But he does not have to live with them.)

Tips for conversing with your husband:

- Stick to the point(s) at hand. (Do not say every thought that enters your mind.)

- Be quick to listen and slow to speak.

- Listen carefully to what he says, without constant interruptions.

- Ask his opinion on things.

- When a thought enters your mind, ask yourself why you want to share it with him. Is it for his benefit or yours?

- Know your husband and how he typically converses with people.

- Learn that silence is not inherently evil.

- Build up, don't criticize.

Stop & Discuss...

+ Husband, is she a good conversationalist? What does she do that encourages and discourages you to want to talk to her?
+ Does she ramble or go down random trails?
+ Wife, do you? Do you see why this could seem disrespectful to him?
+ Husband, is she a good listener? Talk about it.
+ Wife, what do you need to change in your talking habits?
+ Wife, are you critical?
+ Husband, give her an example or two of how she has built you up in conversations.

8. Time to Himself

Most men need a regular time of quiet solace or some other way to refresh and recharge. We may want to think, pray, plan, rest, or just get away from everything else. This is not a lack of love for others. Even Jesus withdrew alone on several occasions. It is just something we need. I can tell you (and Krista will confirm) that my time alone makes our time together far better.

Encourage him by:

+ Freeing him to get alone when he needs to. (Don't complain about his temporary isolation.)

+ Praying for his solitude.

+ Helping him plan for these times.

+ Keeping the kids and other distractions from him (if he stays home).

Stop & Discuss...

+ Husband, do you spend time alone? Is it profitable? Explain.
+ Wife, how can you encourage him to have some alone time? What is your biggest struggle in this area?
+ How did your mothers and fathers handle this?

9. A Wife Who Takes Care of Herself and Her Home

This does not mean that a wife is expected to spend two hours a day at the gym, maintain a daily diet of 600 calories, and look like a supermodel, all while making Martha Stewart and June Cleaver look like incompetent slobs. Any husband who places these kinds of expectations on his spouse does not evaluate his wife the way God does. Still, God did make him to appreciate his wife's beauty and homemaking skills, which is difficult if she makes little or no effort toward them.

Wife, the current American obsession with size-2 bodies is not your standard. God's Word sets your goals, and it places a premium on the inward beauty of your heart. Even where age exercises dominion over your appearance, you can still be gloriously beautiful on the inside (as we saw in chapter 9). But God did design your husband to find you physically attractive and desirable. Who cares what the world thinks? Work hard to become your husband's delight. Labor to be pretty for the man who is sacrificially devoting himself to bless you. Find out what he likes for you to wear and dress accordingly. Deny yourself a few cookies along the way (I did not say "*all* cookies") to maintain an attractive appearance. Stay reasonably healthy in diet and exercise. Do the kinds of things that will draw his eyes and attention to you. Make it easy for him to ignore other pretty women.

An attractive home is also part of a wife's "appearance." *Parade of Homes* is not the goal, but a place of love, joy, peace, and order is. This does not mean that every piece of dust has to be removed the moment it lands upon a cabinet top. But give thought to the "aroma" of your home. Does it invite your husband to be there or make him wish he was elsewhere? Is your life a cluttered mess evidenced by the state of every room of your house? Are you so perfectionistic that your home seems sterile and uninhabited? Do you show yourself to be lazy or diligent? Chaotic or organized? Caring or uncaring? Obsessive-compulsive or living in the real world? Remember the *Proverbs 31 wife*.

I love to be home with my wife. The environment itself woos me. Even more enticing is Krista—her appearance, her smell, her touch, her words, her kisses. All of this is the result of her very intentional and hard work.

How to care for yourself and your home:

+ Study your husband and learn what is attractive to him in your appearance and in your home.

+ *Plan* the "aroma" of your home, regularly evaluating and improving it throughout your marriage.

+ Occasionally ask the Holy Spirit for help in accurately examining your motives and attitude toward your appearance. (Do you strive to impress others beside your husband? Do you care about his opinion? Should you give more or less attention to your health and beauty?)

Stop & Discuss...

+ Husband, tell her how important it is to you that she take care of herself.
+ Discuss what you each want the "aroma" of your home to be like.
+ Husband, describe what she can do to make you want to be home more than anywhere else.
+ Wife, what do you struggle with most in taking care of yourself? Your home?
+ Compare how your mothers took care of themselves and their homes.

10. Sex (and Romance)

Dates, love notes, cards in the mail, romantic text messages, special getaways, etc., are typically thought to flow from the husband to the wife. And that should be the normal direction. However, husbands appreciate being wooed a bit, too. So, wife, bust out that romance-generator now and then and knock his socks off.

Husbands want sex because God designed us to want sex. The erotic desires of human beings are God's creation. He made them for our pleasure and enjoyment. Sex is intended to be more than a raw animalistic pursuit of climax, it is an expression of relational and covenantal love. Nevertheless, the Bible is explicit about the physical pleasure of sex, as we will see in the next chapter.

That husbands desire sex is no news flash, but let me address a couple of things. First, a man who does not desire sex with his wife needs to determine why. If it is medical, he needs to seek a remedy. If it is because of sexual sin, he must repent. If it is due to stress or busyness, he must repent of that sin (he is robbing his wife). If it is due to feelings of guilt or condemnation, he needs to receive the grace of the gospel. Whatever the cause, husband, if you are sexually apathetic, you need to discover why and seek a solution. Most young grooms enter marriage worried about wanting sex too much, not too little. Yet, my counseling experience suggests that a growing number of wives are frustrated by their husband's low sex drive. Husband, do not frustrate your wife.

Second, if your idea of good sex has been defined by the world, Hollywood, and pornography, then you have some work ahead of you to understanding sex as God designed it. But it's worth the effort. Like everything else, when done God's way sex is far superior to the feeble attempts of depraved humanity.

Wife, here are some things you need to know about your husband and sex:

+ **Sex is intensely pleasurable for him physically, but it is much more than physical pleasure.** For a husband, sex is a matter of admiration (the way we spoke of it above). Absolutely nothing says, "You're my hero!" like a vigorously sexual wife. The stereotype is that men are lust-driven animals who crave women's bodies. But it can be far more visceral and emotional than that. A man whose wife longs to be with him sexually feels like he can conquer the world. A sexually fulfilled husband will do anything for his wife. Much like physical affection in public, a sexual wife says to her husband, "I love this man. I desire him. I am blessed to be with him. I delight in his manliness and strength." Actually, it says a whole lot more that defies description. The bottom line is that a man's manhood is tied directly to his sexual expression. You have a major part to play in that.

+ **Your enthusiasm in, and enjoyment of, sex is the key to his pleasure.** Most healthy men have little problem achieving climax. But climax is not his greatest desire. (To be candid, he does not need you for that.) What he wants is to delight in your bodies together as *you*, also, delight in your bodies. If it appears that you are simply "doing your duty," his pleasure will be significantly decreased. Loaning him your girly parts while your head is planning the grocery list will insult him. In fact, you may find that soon after the deed is done, your husband is upset, grumpy, or frustrated. You are thinking, "What does he have to be upset about? He got what he wanted." He is thinking, "That is not what I wanted. Why did she just lie there? Why doesn't she enjoy this? What am I doing wrong? Why doesn't my wife want to be intimate with me?" The difference between "mere sex" and "lovemaking ecstasy" is your zeal and passion.

✦ **Your husband has a big sexual ego.** You've heard of male pride, maybe even seen it up close and personal in your father and/or brothers. But that's nothing compared to male *sexual* pride. Husbands often enter marriage convinced that we are sexual supermen, God's gift to our wife, able to send her to the moon and back with no more than a wave of our hand. As such, the slightest hint that we ever leave her unsatisfied (may it never be!) brings us down to earth, a trip we detest. Even worse is when we apply our magic touch and you flinch with discomfort. Our superegos are damaged when you fail to be transported to the land of euphoria, even when we are the cause of your failure. (That's what sin does to a person.) Be gentle with your husband. Encourage him. Don't overreact to his overreaction. Take a long-term view. He will eventually be humble enough to set aside his pride.

✦ **Give him specific instructions.** He needs it. He cannot read your mind, and his natural sexual instincts will not please you. His body parts are quite different from yours. If he tries to do to you what he would like you to do to him (and he will), you will both wish he hadn't. Please help him by explaining what you like and don't like. Guide him. He will love it if you are specific and explicit.

Sex suggestions:

+ **Learn the importance of your enjoyment and enthusiasm.** Remember, his pleasure is directly proportional to his perception of yours. Get into it. Let go and let him know with your actions, your words, and the look in your eyes. Have fun. Express your enjoyment in obvious ways. Use your words!

+ **Overcome shame and inhibition.** Don't be embarrassed by your body, be naked and unashamed. Sexual confidence from a wife covers a multitude of physical imperfections.

+ **Add some spice.** Think about variety. Try things a little differently. Don't get stuck in a rut. Be creative. Pursue inspired sexuality with him.

+ **Initiate sex with your husband.** Again, it communicates your desire, which heightens his.

+ **Flirt with your husband prior to entering the bedroom (or wherever you make love).** Sexual innuendo, subtle hints, suggestive words, whispering things into his ears that you wouldn't want anyone else to hear, etc., will turn up the heat for both of you. Make this a habit, and he will treat you like a queen, his queen.

+ **Welcome and encourage his sexual advances.** Do not make him feel guilty for his sexual interest. It is how God made him. Invite him to pursue pleasure with you. Remember, you handed him the title to your body on your wedding day (1 Cor. 7). Ask him to make frequent use of his special gift.

+ **Don't just be there in body.** Love him enough to engage mentally and emotionally. Set aside all other thoughts when you are together. Letting your mind wander during sex is more offensive than his lapses during conversations with you (and you know how that feels).

+ **Fight against selfishness.** Sex is best when you are both seeking to please the other. If you are self-centered in or out of the bedroom, it will kill the mood.

+ **Pray for your lovemaking desires and give thanks for them.** God wants you to enjoy sex with your husband, and he wants you to please him. Be grateful for this gift, and ask for help in fulfilling his desires.

Stop & Discuss...

+ Husband, describe how pleasurable sex is for you when she is enthusiastic about it.
+ Would you welcome her to be more flirtatious and sexually provocative outside the bedroom? Explain.
+ Wife, do you know what says "Romance!" to him? Tell him, see what he says.
+ Are you an active sex partner or a passive one? Ask him how you could be more active.
+ Are you willing to direct him in pleasuring you? (This presupposes that *you* are learning what pleases you.) Talk about it.
+ Ask him how you could be a greater blessing to him sexually.
+ Do you need to overcome any sexual inhibitions or shame? Are you willing to do it? Discuss.

13

Sex

For those of you who skipped straight to this chapter, well, you're my kind of people. But I must warn you that sexual joy and intimacy is entirely contingent on how strong you are in the things covered in the first 12 chapters. So back you go! Start at the beginning and let the anticipation for this chapter build to its appropriate climax.

Learn to Be Great Lovers

Sexual attraction is a powerful force. If it wasn't, lust, fornication, and adultery would not be so hard to resist. For we who are married, the time to restrain sexual urges is over, the time to pursue them has begun. This is true whether you have been married for two weeks or two decades. Sex must not be pushed into the corner, swept under the rug, or hidden in the closet. It is a gift from the Lord Jesus, one which He intends you to open happily and regularly.

The art of lovemaking (and it *is* an art) is not the primary topic of this section. I am not going to describe techniques or practices. Consider this not a how-to but a why-to. Still, I commend to you a lifelong enrollment in the *Advanced Studies of Sexual Delight*. Become a master. Better yet, make it a PhD. The more accomplished you become in intimate relations, the more pleasurable your entire marriage will be because the keys to a great sex life are also the keys to a great married life.

Designed to Be Captivating and Constant

There is nothing like sex. At its best, it transcends all other pleasures. Even when less than perfect it is still pretty good. That is how your heavenly Father designed it to be. And He expects you to enjoy it a lot. Here's what He said about it:

> *Let your fountain be blessed,*
> *And rejoice in the wife of your youth.*
> *As a loving hind and a graceful doe,*
> *Let her breasts satisfy you at all times;*
> *Be exhilarated always with her love.*
> *~ Proverbs 5:18-19*

Solomon told his son to rejoice in his wife, then he told him *how* to rejoice in her: by being sexually satisfied with her all the time. Several things are noteworthy about this.

First, a father speaking openly about sex and "private parts" with his son. Many sons today would be shocked to learn that their fathers even knew women had breasts, much less delighted in them, or so it sometimes seems. It is hard to imagine most of the parents I know discussing breasts, penises, clitorises, and orgasms with their adult children. That's unfortunate.

Second, the Bible acknowledges a man's desire for breasts. I love my wife's breasts. Husband, you should, too. (Your own wife's breasts, that is.) They are a beautiful part of the female form designed by God.

Third, the word "satisfy" does not quite capture the Hebrew intent. *Satiate* would be better. To be satiated is to have all you can handle. There is no room for more. You are so full, one more bite would make you explode. Now don't miss this! The Holy Spirit inspired Solomon to instruct his son to receive so much pleasure from his wife's body that he lacks the capacity for any more.

This is also very practical advice. If I am so brimming from my wife's sexual feast that I cannot stand another bite, I will not be looking to nibble from someone else's plate. (Or, as Krista likes to put it, "Feed him well at home and he won't want to eat out.")

Fourth, wife, your husband can only be satiated by your breasts if you make them available. You are to be his sexual "all you can eat" buffet. Make him the fattest man on the planet. You will both find great pleasure in it.

Lastly, this is God's design. He intends for spouses to be sexual gluttons, reveling in bodily, erotic enjoyment.

> *The more accomplished you become in intimate relations, the more pleasurable your entire marriage will be because the keys to a great sex life are also the keys to a great married life.*

Pause for a moment to compare lovemaking with other Christian virtues. Is there an entire biblical book on feeding the hungry? How about attending church? Stewardship? Praying? Teaching? Evangelizing? Now consider that the Holy Spirit inspired a whole book— *Song of Solomon*—with the singular purpose of illustrating God's design for the erotic, sensual, sexual passion of a husband and wife. Sex matters to God. It is offensive and ungrateful to Him when we neglect this wonderful blessing. Don't be negligent and ungrateful!

This is not the place for a full exploration of *Song of Solomon,* but I would draw your attention to a couple of things worth considering the next time you read it. First, the woman is every bit as sexual as the man. She wants it and she's not afraid to say it. She invites her guy to have her and expresses, rather graphically, how she wants to be had. Any view of sex that discourages or shames a woman's erotic desires is an unbiblical one.

Second, both the husband and the wife speak openly about their sexual attraction to the other. We Christians are sometimes shy about admitting that we want and enjoy sex. Don't be shy! Be like the couple in the *Song*. Pursue each other, and talk it up as you do.

Stop & Discuss...

+ Breasts aren't the only satisfying part of a woman's body. Husband, tell her what arouses you about her anatomy.
+ Wife, God created your body to be a source of pleasure for him. You need to get comfortable with that thought. Tell him how it makes you feel to know he desires you.
+ Husband, do you know how God designed her body to work sexually? Have you learned how to bring her to orgasm? Wife, tell him what he does well and what he still needs to work on.
+ Wife, do you want him to pursue you more frequently for sexual pleasure? Explain why or why not.
+ Husband, let her know what indicates willingness or unwillingness to you. What could she do to make herself more sexually available?
+ Pray together and give thanks for body parts, arousal, and sexual pleasure. Ask the Designer of sex for the help that you need.

A Marriage Barometer

According to my iMac's dictionary, a barometer is "an instrument which measures atmospheric pressure, used especially to forecast the weather and determine altitude." I like to say that sex measures a marriage's *relational* pressure (are things easy and loose or hard and tense?), helpful to forecast the *whether* (whether there are unresolved issues) and determine *attitude* (are each of you happy, content, and selfless?). If the two of you are living according to the biblical principles laid out in this book, you should have deeply fulfilling sex, and lots of it. If you have become selfish, lazy, or worldly, sex will be frustrating and rare. Most of the time when couples seek counseling for sexual problems, they are treating the symptom not the cause. A poor sex life is the result of a poor relationship. Thriving, exciting sex is the result of a thriving, exciting marriage.

Unless you have health problems, both of you should desire frequent sex. A husband who feels admired, respected, and wanted by his wife will want to have frequent sex with her. A wife who feels cherished, secure, and loved by her husband will want to make love to him often. God made us this way. He made sex to be the sublimest expression possible of love, unity, intimacy, and pleasure. In my years of counseling marriages, I have never had a couple who struggled in other areas but were sexually passionate and fulfilled.

The Causes of Infrequent Sex

The causes of infrequent sex are many. As I said earlier, they are usually symptoms of broader marital issues that need immediate attention. Below are some of the most common, with brief explanation.

Too tired. Sometimes one or both spouses are not interested because of fatigue or lethargy. Certainly, life does have its weary moments. But too often this is a matter of "too lazy," not "too tired." If you have stopped chasing each other around the bedroom, you have also probably stopped doing many of the other things that make a marriage happy.

Being too tired is usually an indication of selfishness or frustration: *Selfishness,* when one of you is more concerned with your own rest or sleep at the expense of intimacy. *Frustration,* when one of you is discontent with his/her sexual experience and feels exhausted and hopeless (as though the return is not worth the investment).

All of this indicates that you are unwilling to pay the necessary cost of a godly marriage. Watch out! A storm may be brewing.

Stop & Discuss...

+ How often do you use tiredness as a reason for not making love?
+ Strategize together about what changes you can make to overcome tiredness. (Maybe do it earlier in the day. Maybe commit to it on certain days, no matter what.)
+ If either of you needs to confess selfishness, pause and ask for forgiveness now.

Too busy. Many couples struggle to "find time" for lovemaking, especially after the kids start arriving. Let's think about this for a minute. God designed sex to be immensely pleasurable for both spouses. It is the sublimest expression of love possible for human beings. It gives a foretaste of eternal delight with Christ. It is commanded. It is the defining act of marriage. It is one of the keys to a great marriage. And somehow we cannot find time for it?

If you are too busy for sex, you are too busy. Your schedule has become sinfully ordered. Your priorities are unbiblical. Sex is not something to be squeezed into the margins or entrusted to chance. Remember, it is an art. Arts require time for preparation and practice. You must apply yourself to its perfection.

Also remember that your calendar is your slave, not your master. Take charge of your life, ensuring that adequate time is reserved for erotic engagements.

> *Sex matters to God. It is offensive and ungrateful to Him when we neglect, abuse, or minimize this wonderful blessing. Don't be negligent and ungrateful!*

Let me be very candid with you. As I write this, Krista and I have three children, ages 16, 14, and 12. I am the senior pastor of a 500-member (and growing) church, the founder/chairman of a Christian ministry, the president and main teacher of a seminary, an author, a marriage conference speaker, a song-writer and executive producer of several upcoming music projects, and a few other things. Krista is a pastor's wife, a homeschooling mom, the proofreader for all of my writing, a mentor for several women at church, a marriage conference speaker, a percussionist on the music team, a copy editor and freelance writer, and a full-time homemaker. Oh, and, we run a marriage ministry (www.godsdesignformarriage.com). We know busy. We know schedule demands. We know full calendars. And we know sex. Regular, exhilarating, Christ-honoring, passionate sex. It gets better every day. We are constantly studying each other and learning more about how to pleasure the other. We are aggressive and persistent. We have to say no to many things, but we refuse to say no to our marriage. And the results are electrifying. Therefore, we can say from firsthand experience that the "too busy" excuse is just that, an excuse.

Stop & Discuss...

+ If you has used busyness as an excuse, confess and repent. Ask the Holy Spirit for help to change. Now, change!
+ Talk about how your marriage would be better if you invested more time pursuing each other sexually.
+ Discuss what changes you can make to your weekly schedule. (And be sure to actually use the newly created time for lovemaking.)

"Not tonight, I have a headache." There are legitimate health problems which hinder sexual pleasure. If that's true for you, seek the appropriate medical attention so that pleasure can be pursued once again.

But symptoms may be exaggerated or even invented by a spouse, since they seem to be an acceptable excuse for avoiding intercourse. When this happens, either the "ill" partner is being selfish, or there is a problem in the relationship which needs to be addressed.

Stop & Discuss...

+ Are there legitimate health issues affecting your sex life that need attention? Talk about it.
+ Does it seem like your spouse rarely feels well when it comes to lovemaking? Tell them about it (graciously and gently).
+ If you are finding excuses for why you don't want to have sex today, what does that say about your heart and your love for your spouse? Pray, confess, repent, and discuss.

Lack of desire. Again, there may be a medical reason for reduced sexual interest. If necessary, seek medical help. But more common are emotional and relational reasons.

Emotional apathy comes when something else in life has become more significant than the marriage. For example, stress has a major impact on sexual desire. But if a man becomes stressed over his job to the point of sexual disinterest, he has allowed his occupation to occupy too much of his emotional bandwidth. Yes, career is a big deal. But loving his bride is a bigger deal. And, by the way, sex is a great stress-reliever. If you and your spouse enjoy a vigorous sexual relationship, you may find that you can handle just about anything work can throw at you. (The same would be true of an anxious wife. Investigating new ways of driving her husband wild can do wonders for worry.) A man who is too stressed to be sexually engaged and enthusiastic sins against his wife and against his Lord.

If you lack sexual desire because of relational apathy, your marriage is heading for severe turbulence. The only cure is a renewed passion for selfless love, which will bring a renewed passion for sexual love.

I should add a note about pornography here. (I will focus on men, but I know that women struggle with porn, too.) I counsel more and more men who are not interested in sex. Actually, that's not true. He desires sex, just not with his wife. He wants to see a naked body, just not hers. He wants climax, but not with her. She is no longer arousing after watching women with fake bodies portray erotic fairytales. His make-believe world makes reality a bore. She seems unattractive and dull. Because the surgically created girls of his *Fantasy Land* are flawless, the body in his bedroom seems terribly flawed. So he chooses to watch pretend women pretending to have mind-blowing sex (they are acting, remember!) rather than be with a real woman who really wants to have mind-blowing sex. He turns to porn and away from the covenant bride to whom he promised lifelong devotion. The only cure is full repentance. Pastoral help must be sought.

Husband and wife, if pornography is or has been part of your life, please talk to a pastoral counselor about it. This sin will not simply go away on its own. Remember, lust is a *heart* problem. Sex, even in marriage, does not cure a heart problem. It needs the gospel of grace and the Spirit of power.

Stop & Discuss...

+ If either of you believes there is a medical issue causing low sexual desire, discuss it and plan to see a doctor, or pursue another appropriate cure.
+ Discuss the level of stress in your life and marriage. How is it impacting your sexual relationship? What changes are you willing to make?
+ If one or both of you seem to have lower sexual interest than you used to, after ruling out a medical explanation, consider having sex daily for one month. Plan at least one night each week to discuss your sexual desires at length. Talk about it. Do it!
+ If either of you is into porn, are you willing to give it up for the sake of your marriage (not to mention that it's sin)? Seek pastoral counsel and pray for the Spirit's empowerment to enjoy sex only with your spouse.

The Cause of Frequent Sex

The most frequent cause of infrequent sex is selfishness. Conversely, when you selflessly seek to bless each other in and out of the bedroom, sexual bliss will be a regular experience. If you learn what brings erotic gratification to the other, consistent joy follows. If you both apply Christ's axiom "It is better to give than to receive" to sex, you will prove Him right over and over again. I know what I am talking about; I have more than 24 years of experience. When I am only concerned with my own satisfaction, sex is okay for me and bland for my wife. If I try to send her to the moon, we both get there.

> *Sex is designed by God to be immensely pleasurable for both spouses. It is the sublimest expression of love possible for human beings. It is intended to give a foretaste of eternal delight with Christ. It is commanded. It is the defining act of marriage. It is one of the keys to a great marriage. And somehow we cannot find time for it?*

You may have heard the expression, "Sex begins in the kitchen." The idea is that a guy who assists his wife with household duties will find her a willing participant in the bedroom. That is true, but it can sound a bit manipulative, especially for men who hear, "All I have to do to make my wildest dreams come true is help her with the dishes?" I prefer to say it like this: "Marriage should be in a constant state of foreplay." Everything is sexual. Every act, conversation, and encounter is preparation for lovemaking. Flirt incessantly. Make suggestive comments to each other.

Talk about what you did recently, what you might do later, and what you want to try someday. Whisper provocatively in each other's ear. Touch relentlessly.

Krista and I do all of this and more. We show some restraint when people are watching, but when they're not…. Our kids tell us daily to please *stop* kissing and caressing. We don't. We express to each other how much we love to be married, love to be together, love our lives, and love to make love. This spills over into every area of married life. I want to please Krista, to serve her and to fulfill her sexual desires, which instinctively makes me want to fulfill her other desires also. She is my bride, my treasure, my love. I want her to be happy. She does the same for me. Our mutual happiness culminates in happy sexual expression as God intended it to. We live in a constant state of foreplay. I urge you to follow our example.

Another popular expression is, "Men are microwaves and women are crockpots." This means that men can heat up in nanoseconds, but women take all day to warm. We don't find that to be true when sex stays at the forefront of our minds. Sustained affection, provocative discourse, and sensual teasing tend to keep us both ready to go at any moment. Or, to put it another way, water that is always simmering doesn't require much heat to boil.

> *If you both apply Christ's axiom "It is better to give than to receive" to sex, you will prove Him right over and over again.*

Talk About Sex

You can't learn more about each other sexually without talking about it. You need to overcome your inhibitions to discussing it. Be willing to ask specific questions and to give specific answers. (You cannot expect your spouse to read your mind or your body.) Be willing to show and guide each other toward pleasurable areas of touching and kissing and whatever else you are willing to try. Remember, you are to be naked and *unashamed*. That includes being unashamed to talk about what feels good and what doesn't, what you like and don't like, and what you want him/her to do to you. Sex talk should be titillating and fun.

Stop & Discuss...

+ Ask yourself, "How am I selfish when it comes to sex?" then share with the other and ask for forgiveness.
+ Wife, tell him what he could do outside the bedroom that would make you more eager to have sex.
+ What would it take for the two of you to live in a constant state of foreplay? Are you willing to be more like that? Discuss.
+ Are you comfortable discussing sex and body parts? Can you say *penis, clitoris, breast, orgasm*, etc. out loud? (Was that the first time you've said those words in the last year?) What changes are you willing to make to talk more together about sex?
+ Husband, describe in detail something sexual she does that you really like.
+ Wife, your turn. Describe it for him.

Three Kinds of Sex

You probably expect the three kinds of sex to be something like great, amazing, and other-worldly, but that is not what I am talking about. Rather, it's about pace and preparation. I didn't come up with these categories, I don't even know when or where I first heard them, but they have proven helpful in establishing expectations for our sexual experience.

It goes like this:

Fast-Food Sex. You decide on the spur of the moment to eat, and you get to it. In typical sexual lingo, it's "the quickie," no preparation necessary. The goal is not to explore every nuance of sexual consumption, but to enjoy a quick "bite" and then get on with other things. While you should not live on an exclusively fast-food diet, it is a staple for good sexual health (especially with kids at home).

Sit-Down Dinner Sex. Unlike fast-food, this takes time and forethought, and it feeds a bigger appetite. Preparation includes extended conversation about a variety of things (including sex). Usually the atmosphere is important, as is time to warm up before and cool down after. The expectation will be that both spouses participate fully, enjoying deep sexual fulfillment. You won't have time to eat here every day, but strive for at least once a week.

Five-Star Sex. This is the top of the line, luxurious, extravagant kind of sex. It occurs occasionally. It requires much planning and preparation. Often it entails a night or two away with lots of time for unhurried, uninterrupted intercourse (both kinds). It will include prolonged sessions of exploring each other sexually, trying new things, learning more and more about your bodies. The expectation is that because of the extended time without other responsibilities, you both reach the apex of intimacy, fun, companionship, and physical pleasure. This experience will most likely be limited to special celebrations (anniversary, Valentine's Day) and a few other times each year.

Husbands, wives...*eat!* Snack, nibble, linger, binge, dine in, dine out, have a feast, and indulge in the glories of erotic dessert. Do not fast or try to lose weight. Eat! Eat! Eat! It is God's design for you.

Kissing Is Key

During premarital counseling, I ask couples to refrain from kissing until the wedding day. The reason is simple. If they don't kiss, it's highly unlikely they will engage in sexual sin. Think of a car: If I want to drive my car, I need a key with which I can unlock the door, start the engine, put it into gear, and go. Similarly, passionate canoodling is your key to an erotic joyride. Kiss a lot, and I'm don't mean the kind your mother gives you. Let your lips linger regularly before you move on to the other things.

What We Don't Know Can Hurt Us

We are not born with good sexual instincts. This is especially true of men. Men approach sex like they approach everything—*"Full speed ahead!" "Slay the monster!" "Rest is for the weak!" "Only inadequate fools ask for directions!" "Get it done as fast as possible, and dynamite is quicker than digging!"* My wife says that occasionally this can be fun. But, more often, it produces pain and frustration. Women often commit the opposite error, staying *genteel* and *calm* (which sometimes reminds a husband of *asleep*). Instead of guessing or acting out of habit, why not talk about it? Discuss your sexual preferences. Tell each other, before and during, what you're into at the moment. Sex is not supposed to be something either of you merely endures or tolerates.

Plan to Have Sex, Then Do It

Two questions I am asked all the time are: *How often should we be having sex? What's normal?* and *How can we maintain intimacy with children in the home?* Here are my thoughts:

Regarding how often, I can't answer this for every couple since there is no clear biblical instruction. (Though, remember the Bible does use words like: *satiated* and *do not withhold*.) But when people ask, I usually recommend at least four times a week. (If your frequency is considerably lower, that may sound crazy. But trust me, it can be done and then some.)

I usually suggest something like this: pick a weekly *sex date planning time* as a couple, preferably the same time each week. Meet for a few minutes to review the upcoming week and to schedule your sexual dates for the next seven days. Plan at least one "Sit-Down Dinner Sex" event and three "Fast-Food Sex" events each week (see the previous *Three Kinds of Sex* section).

For the Sit-Down event, date night is ideal. If you don't have date night that week, set aside at least an hour for unhurried, mutually satisfying sexual talking and touching. Put the date on the calendar, then plan around it. Tell others *no!* Refuse other invitations because you're "booked" that night at that time. Keep this hour strictly for each other, and enjoy each other's bodies.

For the Fast-Food encounters, be creative. Try some variety. Take a quick "lunch break" together on Saturday afternoon, or during the week if your schedules allow. Set the alarm 15 minutes early on a weekday. Work it in before getting ready to go somewhere or hop in the shower together. Have a post-dinner "discussion" while the kids clean up the kitchen. And there is always the standard quickie in bed before turning out the lights. (There is nothing wrong with that, by the way, as long you guard against laziness and ruts.)

Keep these brief encounters in their proper perspective. They are not designed to create deep intimacy. They are brief connections meant to keep you close to each other so that you don't have far to go when reaching out during the longer connections. Does that make sense? Imagine living together for three weeks without speaking to each other. When you finally do sit down for a couple of hours to talk, there is a lot to sort through before your reach a deep connection. Same thing with sex. If you haven't been together erotically for three weeks, you feel a sense of distance and disconnection that keeps sex from being what it could be. But if you've been connecting sexually on a regular basis, even quickly, the slower encounters start from a place of familiarity and intimacy.

Sometimes I get some pushback on this because scheduling sex seems less romantic and spontaneous. Well sure, it is less spontaneous *by definition*. But in my experience, more planned sex leads to more unplanned sex. The more you do it, the more you both want to do it. As for romance, what could be more romantic than planning an evening of sexual delight and exploration? By knowing it's coming, you can both prepare for the event. You can pray about it. You can let anticipation build in your own heart. You can flirt with and arouse each other throughout the day. You can engage your mind before you engage your body, which usually makes everything more pleasurable. Try it! I doubt you will conclude that it's unromantic.

What about when you have kids in the home? Well, what about it? Have sex! Make time for it. Plan it when the kids are napping. Send them to their room for playtime so you can have your own playtime. Give them a book or let them watch a video. When they're older, tell them that you're going to have some couple time and to leave you undisturbed for the next 15 or 60 minutes. Don't keep your sex life secret from your children. They need to know that in the proper context, it's good and God-pleasing.

One Sunday afternoon when my oldest daughter was about 12, my wife went upstairs to the bedroom. I told my daughter that I needed to talk to her mother for a few minutes, but we would be back shortly. My daughter looked at me with skeptical eyes and hummed, "Mmmmmm hmmmmm!" I smiled and replied, "No, this time we really *are* going to talk. I'll be right back." My kids know what's going on. They frequently tell us to get a room. It's fantastic! They are growing up with a positive view of married affection and sexuality which they will carry into their marriages. Someday, I expect a huge thank you from their spouses. I recommend the same to you. Don't teach your kids through your example that sex is shameful or secret. Show them how to do it God's way (or else they might learn how to do it the world's way).

Stop & Discuss...

+ How often do you kiss, like *really* kiss? Discuss. Now set a timer for 60 seconds and kiss until it goes off.
+ What is your current ratio of Fast-Food sex to Sit-Down Dinner sex? Which do you want more of? Why?
+ Have you ever done a sex getaway for a couple of nights? Would you like to? Talk about it. (Maybe plan one.)
+ Talk about how fun it could be to plan sex dates.
+ Pause right now and plan your next week of sex dates.
+ If you're really adventurous, agree to have sex every day for three months and then reevaluate how often you would like to have sex together.

Know Her Cycle (Yes *That* One)

Years ago, I began to observe certain things about my marriage and our sexual experience, and I discovered some repeatable patterns in Krista's menstrual cycle and desire. As we have discussed this with other couples and pursued more research, it appears to be generally true among women. It's not quite as simple as data in/data out, but on the other hand, it is called a "cycle" for a reason. I encourage you both to consider how this might help your relationship.

It seems that there are four distinct phases in the monthly cycle. I will list them below along with a few reflections. By the way, some wives are so consistent you could make a calendar out of them. For others, it's more like predicting the weather – lots of "could be," "might be," and "percent chance" language. Use this as a starting place, but the goal is to know your wife.

The Period (Days 1-8)

This is one of the two phases that most men seem to know about (the other being PMS). We know this one because it usually means no sex due to bleeding. She does not feel good physically during this phase. She has cramps, pains, and other discomfort. She may be emotionally up and down, feeling tired or irritable, especially the first few days. It's a cloudy and cold stretch. But toward the end, the clouds begin to break apart, and a few rays of sunshine find their way through. Things begin to look up.

I have found that lots of hugs, gentleness, and verbal encouragement have a huge impact on Krista during this time. Soft affection coupled with kind, hopeful words will help her feel loved and cherished. And praying for her with her is great. I will sometimes pray specifically about what is going on in her body and ask for special grace to overcome. God is faithful, frequently granting her joy in serving Him even when her body fights against her.

Ovulation (Days 9-14)

Or, as I prefer to call it, the *Woohoo!! Stage*. This is not only the time when women *can* make babies, it's also when they *want* to make babies. Jesus designed them that way, and He gave them all the things that go with it. Their thoughts, emotions, and bodies all agree—let's do this! Their hormones are raging in a good way. This is the week she feels best. She has energy and seeks engagement. She is rational and less emotional (you know, for a woman). She is sexually eager and enthusiastic. Simply put, it's a fun week in every way.

Week 3 (Days 15-21)

This is the transition stage, heading toward PMS. Early on the wife feels pretty good (though not as good as the previous week), but the clouds are on the horizon. This stage largely resembles the ovulation phase, but everything gradually moves from a ten (or, at times, eleven!) to three or four. For the most part, both her psyche and her body seem largely unaffected by hormones and "the cycle."

PMS (Days 22-28)

"Mostly cloudy with thunderstorms likely" seems like a good way to put it. This is when a woman is most tempted to irritability, laziness, emotional fluctuations, lack of self-control, sinful words, etc. Physically, her status moves between poor and awful. Sexually, she is far less interested, which make sense because her body is saying, "Okay, looks like we are not making a baby. Let's clean up the factory and get it ready for next time."

There was a day when I gave little credence to PMS, and I also gave little grace to Krista. But now I get it, at least as far as a man can. I understand that lying behind much of what she says and does is a hormonal change taking place. While PMS does not excuse sin and selfishness, it does explain some of it. Knowing this helps me stay patient with Krista. It helps me to lead and protect her. It keeps me from offering a solution when she cries, or rather, it helps me understand that the best solution is a long hug followed by expressions of love and appreciation. It helps me help her fight the real enemy—her body, and the devil who seeks to exploit her weakness.

As Krista will tell you, my leadership of and love for her has never been more obvious or effective. In this most practical way, I know my wife deeply. She lives in her cycle every single day. Understanding how it works helps me to walk with her in it every single day. Husband, I urge you to dive into this strange part of your wife's being and get to know who she is at a deeper level.

Specifically regarding sex, knowing this cycle can help establish proper expectations. For example, a wife will typically be most sexual and erotically adventurous during ovulation. She may take the initiative more during those days. She will probably have a much easier time achieving orgasm. But during the PMS week, she may require a slower approach, needing more affection and conversation before sexual touch.

Most guys want to stay as far away from this topic as possible, but husband I would urge you to know your wife's cycle. Stay informed. It may help you decode some of the mystery surrounding her sexual peaks and valleys. Give it a try and see what you learn.

Stop & Discuss...

✦ Are either of you ashamed or put off by the menstrual cycle? Maybe it's time to get over it. God designed it, after all.

✦ Wife, help him understand what you need most during the PMS and period weeks.

✦ Wife, do you notice increased sexual desire during ovulation? Discuss it.

✦ Husband, ask any questions you may have about the menstrual cycle.

✦ Some people avoid sex during ovulation to prevent pregnancy. However, this may deny a woman her most sexually satisfying experiences. If you do this, talk about how you might change your approach to allow for the greatest sexual enjoyment.

Here are a few more quick recommendations for you:

+ Read *Song of Solomon* aloud together. Use it to find greater freedom of sexual expression. Make up your own metaphors to describe each other's body. Write your own erotic poetry.

+ Maintain a sense of humor.

+ Have fun. Sex is supposed to be fun.

+ Experiment. Try new things. Create. Think outside the bed.

+ Talk about sex a lot—before, during, and after the act itself.

+ Pray regularly about and for your lovemaking. (Yes, it is okay to pray about sex. You can even pray explicitly and use words like "desire" and "orgasm" and "clitoris." God won't blush. He designed all those things.)

+ Reread and discuss the sex sections of this book every year.

14

Other Resources and Recommendations

Here, in list form, are more suggestions for your marriage:

1. Read the following books:

   ✦ *The Complete Husband* by Lou Priolo (husband)

   ✦ *Sex, Romance, and the Glory of God* by C.J. Mahaney (husband)

- *Feminine Appeal* by Carolyn Mahaney (wife)

- *Romancing Your Husband* by Debra White Smith (wife)

- *Sheet Music* by Kevin Leman (both)

2. Sometime in the next couple of years, work your way through this book again. You don't need to discuss every question, but talk about the major topics in each section.

3. Ideas I have heard for fun sexual motivation:

- Get a jar and put a penny in it each time you make love for a year. Then take one out each time during the next year (try to empty the jar before the year ends).

- Put a dollar in a jar each time you have sex. See how quickly you can afford a romantic vacation for two.

4. Find a couple who has been married for at least 20 years and who appears to have a joyful, Christ-honoring marriage. Ask them to meet with you every two weeks for the next six months. Ask them about their story, tell them yours, and let them speak into your marriage. Ask them to enter into a prayer agreement that you will pray for each other's marriage daily throughout those six months.

5. Plan a monthly budget together. Allocate (at least) 10% to your church and 10% to savings. Also, be sure to assign some money for dates, getaways, and anniversary events.

6. Go to our website and implement the 4 Foundation Stones of the *Marriage Mansion*: www.godsdesignformarriage.com.

7. Remember—*A cherished woman wants to please her husband*. Memorize that and believe it. It will be the difference between marital bliss and marital blah.

45455198R00144

Made in the USA
San Bernardino, CA
29 July 2019